STRENGTH TRAINING & CONDITIONING FOR BASKETBALL

STRENGTH TRAINING & CONDITIONING FOR BASKETBALL

FEATURING
RALPH SAMPSON'S TRAINING PROGRAM

WILLIAM H. DUNN WITH ERNST H. SOUDEK AND JOE GIECK

Contemporary Books, Inc.
Chicago

Library of Congress Cataloging in Publication Data

Dunn, W. H. (William H.)
    Strength training and conditioning for basketball

    Includes Index
        1. Basketball—Training.   2. Weight lifting.
3. Physical education and training.   4. Sampson,
Ralph, 1960–   5. Basketball players—United
States—Case studies.   I. Soudek, E. H. (Ernst H.)
II. Gieck, J. (Joe)   III. Title.
GV885.35.D86   1984   796.32'32   84   -19903
ISBN 0-8092-5375-5

This book is dedicated to:
—*the athletes on the University of Virginia's men's and women's intercollegiate basketball teams.*
—*the dedicated men and women who make up the National Strength and Conditioning Association, Inc.*
—*members of the National Strength Research Center in Auburn, Alabama.*
—*David F. Cooke, Sr.*
—*especially to Mr. Phil Wendel, without whose encouragement and help, this book would not have been written.*

Photography provided by:

Julie Heyward
P.O. Box 6351
Charlottesville, Virginia 22906

Jon C. Golden
2323 Crestmont Ave.
Charlottesville, Virginia 22903

Cover Photography by Julie Heyward.

Published by Contemporary Books, Inc.
180 North Michigan Avenue, Chicago, Illinois 60601
Manufactured in the United States of America
Library of Congress Catalog Card Number: 84-19903
International Standard Book Number: 0-8092-5375-5

Published simultaneously in Canada by Beaverbooks, Ltd.
195 Allstate Parkway, Valleywood Business Park
Markham, Ontario L3R 4T8 Canada

CONTENTS

Terry Holland, head basketball coach of the University of Virginia Cavaliers.

FROM THE DESK OF TERRY HOLLAND

Every basketball player wants to be the best he possibly can be. Recently, basketball players and coaches at the highest levels of competition have come to realize the value of strength training in the total development of the basketball player.

However, until Coach Dunn arrived at the University of Virginia in 1978 we had no one who could tie a total program together for our athletes and coaches. It is certainly much more than a coincidence that Virginia's basketball team won the National Invitational Tournament in New York the next year.

The programs that Coach Dunn designs are built upon individual needs for specific skills. Our players consistently increase their muscle mass, vertical jump, shooting range, trunk strength, and endurance even during the season. A few years ago most coaches thought strength training would tighten up a player and possibly hurt his shooting. We have found, however, that our shooting percentage has improved since we adopted what has now come to be known as the "Virginia Strength Training and Conditioning Program for Basketball."

This book leaves nothing out, it covers the complete training spectrum better than any which I have ever read. In addition, it is a very timely and needed piece of resource material and one which is my privilege to highly recommend to coaches, athletes, trainers, and to parents wanting expert guidance for their youngsters.

Terry Holland
University of Virginia
Head Basketball Coach

Triumph! Lee Raker (left) and All-American Jeff Lamp embrace after Virginia wins the National Invitational Tournament.

FOREWORD

YOU CAN'T BUY HEART

by Senator Bill Bradley

Five people live and share an unusual communion: achieving unity but not at the expense of individual imagination. You are really betting on the human spirit as much as on mechanical skills. In a day when many workers get paid eight hours' wages for six hours' work, when many politicians ignore the needs of their constituents, and when a lot of policemen fail to show up for a black-out emergency call, why should basketball players be different? A few will loaf, but the contrast between them and members of a well-blended team is stark. Those who have ever played on a **team** never forget the excitement of their work or the fulfillment of a championship. Those who have watched on the night of a final game must sense that they have witnessed ultimate cooperation, that they have seen an unusual kind of sharing, that they have glimpsed a better world—one unattainable outside the arena.

ACKNOWLEDGMENTS

The authors are indebted to and wish to express sincere gratitude to the following individuals who have provided significant contributions in the preparation of this manuscript: Barbara Dunn, Ingrid Soudek, Henry Wingate, Dr. Fred Hatfield, Dr. Frank McCue, Sue Halstead, Dr. Mike Stone, and Jeff Everson.

In particular, we wish to thank John Gamble, assistant strength coach and World Powerlifting Champion, on whose unswerving dedication and expertise much of the success of the University of Virginia strength programs depend.

INTRODUCTION

The strength and conditioning programs that Coach Dunn has developed and I have used have been a great benefit to me as a basketball player.

They have helped me to build a much higher degree of overall body strength and stamina, as well as increased my ability to hold position under the basket, rebound, increase speed and agility, and added several inches to my vertical jump and nearly thirty pounds of solid body weight.

The programs have helped all phases of my basketball game.

This book by Coach Dunn covers all of these programs in great detail and I am proud to recommend it for everyone who wants to improve his skills.

Ralph Sampson
Center, Houston Rockets
1984 Rookie of the Year
1981 & 1982 NCAA Player of the Year

Strength Coaches Bill Dunn (far left) and John Gamble (far right) with some aspiring athletes.

1
GETTING OFF TO A GOOD START

Basketball is a game of high speed and non-stop action, requiring a high level of mental readiness as well as specialized physical skills such as shooting, rebounding, passing, jumping, and running. It is also a game in which performance level is closely linked to an unswerving commitment to personal discipline and improvement.

Whether you are an athlete or a coach, this book will show you step by step, how to develop and implement the very same strength training and conditioning program used by 7'4" superstar Ralph Sampson.

Getting off to a good start demands that two key factors regarding strength training/conditioning for basketball be clearly understood:

1. The basic prerequisite is every athlete's willingness to make the year-round sacrifices required by a strength training and conditioning program which focuses maximum attention on every conceiv-

able factor affecting basketball performance.

2. While skill is unquestionably the major factor in determining the level of success that can be achieved, and although basketball players cannot be "created" in a weightroom, proper strength training with comprehensive conditioning, coupled with sound sportsmedical direction, is the best possible way for you to improve your skill.

The primary purpose of this book is to examine closely exactly how an athlete has to prepare, both physically and mentally, in order to realize his or her maximum potential for success. In so doing, we will focus on the incredible development of the Houston Rockets' Rookie of the Year and University of Virginia's two-time NCAA Player of the Year, Ralph Sampson—an athlete many observers believe will one day be the greatest basketball player who has ever lived.

1

SPORTSMEDICINE FOR BASKETBALL

Two or three weeks before the team starts its workouts, each player should be given a thorough physical examination by the team physician or, in the absence of such a specialist, a family doctor.

Whenever possible, that is, whenever there is a certified trainer or a local sportsmedicine clinic available, each athlete should be scheduled for a comprehensive testing and evaluation session as well.

The procedures involved in these tests should determine the strength, flexibility, endurance, and muscle mass. A deficiency in any of these areas greatly increases the likelihood of injury, thus causing you to begin workouts with a handicap. A disadvantage of this kind will almost invariably hold back progress in the development of basketball skills.

In addition, these strength and fitness testing procedures should cover muscle or joint tightness, as well as various flexibility (range of motion) tests and measurements. Cardiovascular fitness tests such as the twelve-minute run and interval sprints will be outlined and discussed in detail in the chapter on conditioning. These barometers of general athletic fitness should always be included in the testing process of basketball players.

If at all possible, these tests should be conducted at regular intervals throughout the school year because achieving strength increases without improvement or retention of muscle balance and flexibility would be self-defeating.

WHAT WILL BE EXPECTED OF YOU

For junior and senior high school teams and collegiate teams, the period just after classes begin in the fall, and again, at the time immediately prior to embarking on off-season workouts, and finally, just before the players leave school for the summer are the times for large-scale strategic team meetings. These informative and motivational meetings are under the direction of the head basketball coach and involve all personnel associated with the physical development of the team. Reflecting the coach's philosophy, meetings of this kind will tell you:

1. Exactly what is going to be expected of you.
2. Precisely how to discipline yourself to induce maximum adaptive change in your body.

Also, before workouts begin, you should learn about your body, particularly your muscles. Learn the names, locations, and functions of the muscles you'll be developing. You must gain a clear understanding of the basic anatomy of your body as it pertains to basketball performance. In addition, you must learn how speed, strength, and endurance affect your play and how each component may be improved.

Ralph Sampson demonstrates the proper way to do machine lat pulldowns. Note that he keeps his back slightly arched and his elbows thrust down and back for maximum exercise benefit.

2
TRAINING EQUIPMENT

Safety is of the utmost importance, both in and out of the weightroom. All strength training equipment can be dangerous, regardless of whether it is bars, dumbbells, or machines. Improper training techniques, poor spotting practices, or inadequate warm-ups can all produce serious injuries. Therefore, you must become familiar with the weightroom equipment and rules, especially as the latter pertain to safety.

Some of the most obvious rules for safety are:

1. Never train alone.
2. Do not crowd others who are working out.
3. Do not drop bars or plates.
4. Always replace everything used.
5. Never bring food, drinks, or ice bags into the facility.
6. Wear shoes and workout clothes at all times.
7. Observe any guidelines of desired behavior posted by your coach.

In addition, someone must regularly check all equipment to be absolutely sure that it is in proper working order. Regarding the training room, all athletes should be made familiar with the rehabilitation services (e.g., modalities, therapeutic exercise, massages, etc.) it offers. A few helpful hints and guidelines from the trainer can build confidence and commitment on the athlete's part.

THE FACILITY

When considering existing space as a possible strength training facility, particular thought should be given to:

- Structural integrity (floors/walls) and ceiling height (at least 9')
- Adequate ventilation
- Room temperature and temperature control
- Accessibility
- Availability of water, restrooms, showers, and lockers
- Lighting
- Ease of movement from station to station
- Upkeep and cleanliness

5

If adjustments are necessary or if corners must be cut, such changes must not be in the area of safety. Always remember that young lives are involved. Along with this precautionary measure, just a little imagination will show that many possibilities for a training facility exist. Anything from a basement, a garage, or a backyard shop to any number of rooms already existing within the confines of a grade school, a high school, or a college will serve the purpose.

An excellent way to decorate a school or university room is to ask the art department to paint a series of dynamic murals as a class project, depicting a wide variety of athletic activities.

Allowing the entire student body to participate in selecting a name for the facility (ours is called "The Grizzly Den") is a very effective motivational tool which helps build team unity along with school spirit. This is especially true when several different teams are training in the room. The name selected should be painted on the walls—in school colors, of course.

Getting the local boosters club and interested community members involved in the project will help. Often an advertisement in the local or school newspaper will turn up important donations such as:

- Lighting
- Mirrors
- Paint
- Carpet
- Motivational or instructional boards
- Stereo system

A lot of people would like to help. Enthusiasm needs to be built—it's contagious.

EQUIPMENT FOR THE TRAINING ROOM

Because many facilities are not large and because the three primary criteria are: Is it safe? Is it functional? And is it affordable? We strongly suggest that you, your teammates, parents, and friends make most of the equipment needed. Naturally, the ideal situation is for businesses in the community to donate the necessary material for the shop to make what is needed, but even if the cost of these materials must be absorbed, you will still come out ahead, as new equipment is expensive.

Some of the necessary equipment which cannot be built can be donated as well. Building as much of the equipment as possible allows you to tailor the training room to your own requirements and use the space efficiently. This can rarely (if ever) be accomplished if standard merchandise is purchased.

The accompanying diagram shows our suggestion for the arrangement of equipment and the specific pieces needed to implement our program. In developing this illustration we have taken into consideration the fact that in nearly all school situations other athletes in addition to basketball players will be training there.

Obviously, this room (see page 7) and the accompanying equipment can be scaled down or up depending on specific needs. For example, in the case of the basement weightroom, only one power rack and flat bench would be needed.

Some of the equipment shown here can be made; other pieces must be purchased or donated. The meaning of the various abbreviations is as follows:

AC	Air conditioners (2)
BNP	Behind neck pulldown (Lat machine) (1)
CB	Chalk boxes (2)
CS	Curl station (1)
DBR	Dumbbell rack with assorted bells
DS	Dip station (1)
FB	Flat bench press bench (1)
HC	Hamstring curl machine (1)
HL	Hanging ladder (1)
IB	Incline bench with upright (1)
KE	Knee extension machine (1)
OLP	Overhead lifting platform (1)
PB	Sets of pulling boxes (3)
PR	Power racks (2)
SR	Seated row machine (1)
TB-R	Toe board with hand rail (1)
W	Windows (3)
WF	Water fountain (1)
WH	Weight holders (4)

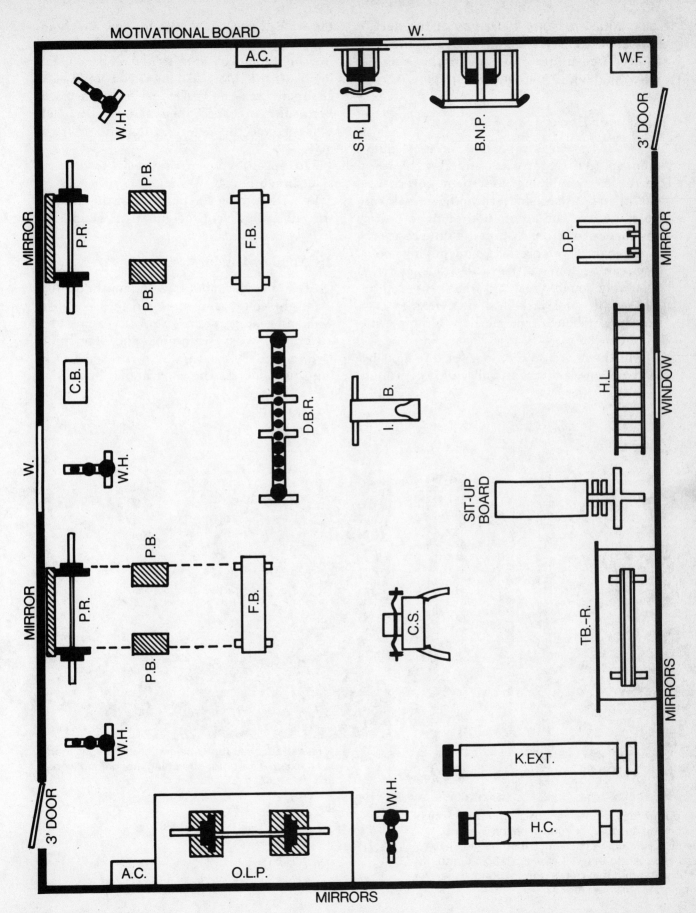

Let's take a closer look now at the necessary equipment. Keep constantly in mind that safety precautions must never be omitted when making or purchasing equipment.

1. Power Racks (two)

This is the most important piece of equipment in any weightroom, and also the most versatile. By building your own, the cost is cut in half. Also, since the power rack can hold the bar, the acquisition of huge power benches for the bench press is unnecessary.

All manner of pressing and pulling exercises can be done on the power rack, and in a relatively small area. All that's needed in addition to the rack and the weights is a sturdy flat bench, and perhaps a simple incline bench.

Bolt the rack into the floor (or into an 8' by 10' wooden platform) and all the way through the walls if possible. Holes for the steel holding pins (to support the weights) must be 1⅛" in diameter and must be spaced 3" apart (starting 6' off the floor). Tubing used should be 3" channel iron. The rack must be at least 7'8" high, and the space between the two left uprights and the two right uprights must be 5'.

The space between the uprights on each side should be 24".

Be sure to turn the pins (six of them) up at the ends to prevent weights from sliding.

2. Wooden Ladder

A plain ladder, about 12' in length, painted in bright colors and mounted into both the wall and ceiling at a height of 8' is a must for abdominal work, chinning, and stretching. Use very heavy bolts and screws when attaching this ladder to the walls and ceiling.

The power rack is a tremendously versatile piece of equipment, suitable for squats, bench presses, deadlifts, and chin-ups. Notice that the rack has been attached to the wall as well as bolted into the ground and that a mirror is present so that the user can monitor his own form.

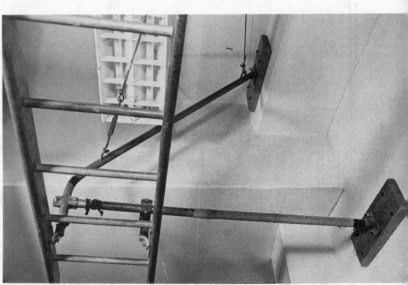

A ladder attached to the ceiling of the weight room is an excellent tool for stretching, abdominal work, and chin-ups.

Weight holders occupy a small area and help keep the weight room clean and uncluttered.

A toe board and handrail are simple to install and great for stretching and strengthening the calves.

3. Weight Holders

In the weightroom diagram we suggest making at least four of these very practical weight holders. They are easily made, occupy a small area, last for years and, when painted (stem and rim only), are very attractive.

4. Chalk Boxes

Two attractive boxes to hold the chalk (magnesium carbonate) will be ample. These are easily kept up and can be quickly made from standard lumber, and almost any sturdy legs will suffice. Again, paint these in very bright colors. They can be any size as long as they are at least 6" to 8" deep.

5. Toe Board and Hand Rail

This is a great way to exercise the calf muscles, which require high repetitions.

6. Dip Station

This piece of equipment must be bolted through the wall, not on it, as well as into the floor or on a small platform.

For the best grip glue a coarse brand of sandpaper onto the bar at the grip position.

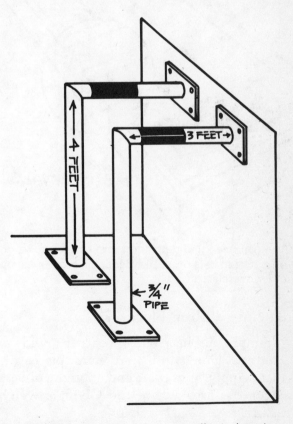

A parallel bar dip station is an excellent place to develop the triceps.

Paint the entire station in bright colors. This is a very inexpensive but important piece of equipment.

7. Overhead Lifting Platform

This platform is a must and has many uses. Do not paint it; instead, apply three applications of "gymcoat," the same solution used to preserve basketball gym floors and make them shine.

Be sure to leave a crack between the top layer boards and use heavy lumber. The rubber floor can be old door mats, conveyor belts, old tires, or any type of rubberized flooring, as long as it is strong. Nail it down tight after the platform has been stained. One of these will be sufficient.

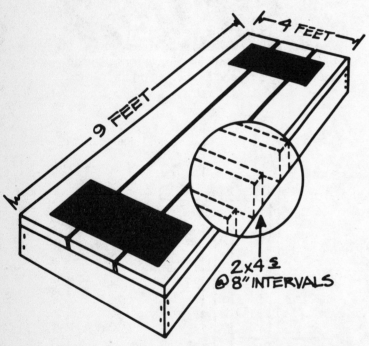

The overhead lifting platform is used to rest weights on between sets of cleans, deadlifts, high pulls, and other exercises.

8. Four Pulling Blocks

Simply purchase one 8′ board 10″ wide and 2″ thick. Cut it into four equal pieces of 2′ each. Apply "gymcoat" and enough rubber to cover the area where the Olympic weights will rest.

These blocks should be stored in a corner near the power racks when not in use. When power cleans, high pulls, dead lifts, etc., are to be trained, just put the blocks out in front of the power racks and set the Olympic bar(s) on them. The blocks save a lot of space and are much less expensive than additional platforms, not to mention protecting the floor from possible damage.

Nearly all major exercises can be safely performed in this area with a minimum of equipment and expense.

Equipment You Can Buy

Over the years we have shopped around considerably. We have tried nearly everything. Of the many fine companies we have done business with and whose equipment we currently have in the UVA varsity weightroom, four stand out above the rest in our opinion. We would like to recommend:

York Barbell Company
P.O. Box 1707
York, PA 17405
Speak to: Mr. John Terpak (Jr. or Sr.)
(717) 767-6481

AMF American
200 American Avenue
Jefferson, IA 50129
(Ask for: Dir. of Product Service)
(800) 274-3978

Qualiform, Inc. (Bumpers USA)
350 State Street (P.O. Box 28)
Wadsworth, OH 44281
Speak to: Nick Antonio—Owner
(216) 336-6777

Wright Weight Equipment
6510 1st Avenue
Birmingham, AL 35206
Speak to: Leo Wright—Owner
(205) 591-6564

In programs starting from scratch, the following is the remainder of the necessary equipment, which can be either donated or bought.

- Olympic weights, three sets, 400 pounds each
- Olympic plates, 1,000 pounds, various sizes
- Flat benches with no uprights, two
- Heavy-duty incline bench
- Hamstring curl/knee extension machine
- Seated row machine
- Lat machine (floor model)
- Dumbbells (assorted) and Holder. We suggest plate welded with revolving grips.

Even if the cost for all of the equipment which we have listed must be absorbed, the final cash outlay is still under $4,000 including all accessories such as lighting, carpet, paint, and mirrors. Raising such a sum should be relatively easy in any program that has school and community involvement.

In the case of a basement workout area, a little hard work (cutting grass, washing cars, shoveling snow, etc.) can turn up enough money to purchase the materials for:

- one power rack
- one hanging bar (or ladder)
- one weight holder
- one flat bench
- three or four pairs of dumbbells
- toe board, dip station
- one set of weights

Then, along with your friends or parents, you can make everything for about $600. When Christmastime or birthdays roll around, why not ask for the extras you want?

Hitting the books after pumping iron: Keeping a record of their progress is a must for athletes who plan on winning.

3

MOTIVATION AND MENTAL PREPARATION

Not long ago, at a leading basketball camp attended by over 600 aspiring youngsters, one of the nation's finest basketball coaches made the following statement: "How many of you would like to be great athletes?" Almost instantly six hundred hands went up. "Good. What then would you give or trade for such an honor?" No hands this time.

After a you-could-hear-a-pin-drop silence, the legendary coach remarked again, "How many are not sure but would appreciate a little help in finding out?" Again the hands shot up.

"Good," he said again, "that will be the goal and the purpose of this camp." And, we might add, of this chapter.

Motivation plays an all-important part in basketball. But so often this elusive "factor of the mind" appears to mean something different to everyone. You may participate in basketball for one reason, your friend for another reason. That's okay, because what-ever makes *you* tick is what will help make you a good athlete.

THE ATHLETE'S RESPONSIBILITY

The 19th-century English poet, Robert Browning, once wrote that "A man's reach should exceed his grasp," and we believe that this would be an excellent philosophy for any basketball player.

Certainly an athlete who says, "This is my limit: I cannot progress any further," has indeed reached his limit. The great UCLA basketball coach John Wooden said it this way: "Do not ever let your mind limit what your body can achieve." This is not to say that there is not a place in basketball for such a player. This "recreational attitude" may be a fine way to just relax and have some fun, but it hardly lends itself to any major improvement or advancement.

In order to "focus in" even better on the

responsibility of the player, let's look closely at the following thoughts:

- Winning is a very wholesome objective, yet very few really know how to go about it. The will to win has always been grossly overrated as a means of doing so, because everyone wants to win. The will to prepare to win and the ability to prevent losing are of far greater importance.—Bobby Knight

- The most valuable result of all education is the ability to make yourself do the thing you have to do, when it ought to be done, whether you like it or not.—Author unknown

- Take the best team and the worst team and line them up. You will find very little difference physically. But there is a difference. The winners have a very special dedication. . . . They will not accept defeat.—Merlin Olsen

Participants in virtually all athletic contests which end in a loss, and in which the outcome is not a foregone conclusion, have always known that they were not defeated so much by the opposition as by the fact that they found a way to beat themselves.

The question, then is how this negative factor may be reversed. How may the all-important "will to prepare to win" be developed? Furthermore, how can a player acquire or develop the ability to prevent losing, or ideally, how can a player arrive at a state of mind that will not at any time succumb to defeat?

Success is difficult to define, and harder to achieve. You must be able to determine what constitutes success, what sort of commitment you are willing to make, and how you will establish and achieve your goals.

Perhaps an example will help here. All of us can remember, after observing a great player in action, thinking something like, "Ah, yes, if I were seven feet tall or had that kind of speed," or "If I had a body like that . . . well, then I would really be something!"

At first glance, nothing seems particularly wrong with such reasoning. However, successful athletes channel their thoughts in a more positive direction, one that helps them come to grips with the fact that they aren't somebody else and never will be, and like it or not, they will have to build on the material they do possess. The sooner you face this fact instead of wallowing in the mire of wishful thinking, wishing you were someone else or that you had the specific advantages that somebody else has, the sooner you will be able to get on with something productive— like striving with all your might to become all that your own potential will allow.

This can be accomplished by constantly reinforcing a self-image of strength, of positively channeled aggressiveness, and of mental toughness. When looking in awe at the great superstars, you should try to get a deeper appreciation of the vastness of your own abilities and potential. Acquire the ability to follow the great athletes' examples. Realize that what you are actually witnessing is not someone born great but the culmination of maximum long-term effort. You are not now, nor will you ever be, Ralph Sampson. But you can follow his good example, and learn from his actions.

And last, keep in mind that the ability to prevent losing and to achieve a state of mind which will not succumb to defeat are developed in training. Proper diet, adequate rest and recovery, total commitment, comprehensive training practices, and, at game time, instantly and relentlessly applied pressure, will force the opponent to reach every level of fatigue long before you begin to tire.

When such a price has been paid in physical training and mental preparation, succumbing to defeat will not be your problem. Arriving at this realization is the beginning of mental toughness—the initial step in "right thinking." True motivation in action is actually mental toughness on display. The greatest struggle, one more important than that indicated on any scoreboard, is the one within ourselves. It is the outcome of this daily conflict which determines the person we are

Pushing it to the max! Professional basketball star Jeff Lamp trains to win with seated incline bench presses, which exercise the deltoids and triceps.

The agony and intensity of maximum effort show on the face of this athlete, here pictured doing pullovers, a great exercise for back muscles.

becoming everyday throughout the course of our lives. You must strive to develop a positive frame of mind in order to be successful. You must look within yourself for the answers.

THE COACH'S RESPONSIBILITY

On the surface, it is the responsibility of the strength and conditioning specialists to provide athletes with sound training programs and technique instruction, plus encouragement, direction, and leadership consistent with the head coach's philosophy—all in such a manner and in an atmosphere that will be conducive to each athlete's long-term success. It is below the surface, however, that the coach's true value, as well as his ultimate responsibility, comes to light. A coach must always do everything within his power to see that athletes clearly understand the true meaning of success and failure. Developing a team's physical talent and potential for success is one thing, and an important one, but helping to mold young and impressionable minds is far more important than scoreboards, and requires consummate understanding, tact, and skill.

SETTING GOALS THAT GUARANTEE SUCCESS

There is a saying that goes "yard by yard it is awfully hard, but inch by inch it becomes a cinch." Breaking down any long-term task or goal into smaller, more attainable parts is always conducive to achievement and success, and helps to crystalize in your mind a basic overview of the entire year. Yet weightrooms everywhere are filled with hopeful young athletes who have little or no idea where their training is taking them. They envision a magnificently honed body and finely tuned athletic skills, but they have no inkling of a systematic approach that will advance them towards that goal.

The Yearly Overview Chart

Developing a Yearly Overview Chart (like the one shown on page 17) will give you a long-term plan, and will help you to set goals. If you stick with the chart, you'll be able to track your progress and determine what you want to achieve.

Note that the chart is divided into three parts, representing both the periods of preparation and the competitive basketball season. Each 11-week segment on the chart indicates a "cycle" with three distinct phases. The specifics of these phases will be discussed in subsequent chapters.

Establish specific goals on a daily, weekly, monthly, and annual basis. At this time, a coach or parent can be of invaluable assistance to you, particularly if you're just starting out.

Select poundages that can be comfortably handled for all repetitions, not allowing partial movements, and do not sacrifice good form. If necessary, start with just the bar and no added weights.

In formulating these goals, you must know where you stand at the outset. Use two or three workouts to determine good starting points. Record your vertical jump and your previous best performance on dips, chins (palms out), thirty-second jump rope (each foot and both feet), distance for standing long jump times ten, and abdominal hangs, plus other exercises which will be discussed in later chapters. This may sound like a great deal of work, but it is worth every second it requires.

REST AND RECOVERY

Both mental and physical rest and recovery are among the most important requirements of outstanding basketball performance, because a tired player is inefficient and injury-prone. Any hard workout requires at least 48 hours of recovery. This is one reason basketball games are spaced apart. You need time to rest both before and after a demanding game or workout. However, "rest" and "recovery" are not necessarily synonymous with "lying around" and "doing nothing." Rather, these terms imply active rest and active recuperation, which mean that you should engage in non-strenuous physical activity (stretching, table tennis, short hikes) to give the muscles a sharp edge. Likewise, "rest" should not be interpreted as "switching off" mentally. Some of the great champions believe that at those times when their bodies are at rest their minds should be working. Playing a mentally demanding game, such as chess, is a great way to retain mental sharpness while physically recovering. Reading and studying fulfill the same purpose, and in the long run serve the student athlete even better.

Success can be gained only through sacrifice in terms of training and lifestyle. Sleeping habits, for instance, vary with each individual, as do sleeping needs, but there is enough medical evidence to indicate that a minimum of eight hours of sleep a night is a must for players in high school or college. Nine or ten hours of sleep are even better.

The player who consistently gets insufficient sleep does not give his or her body time to recuperate. In addition, smoking, drinking, or drug use are certainly harmful to an athlete (and others as well!) and must not be tolerated. Not only will you cheat yourself, but you'll also cheat your team of having you playing at your full potential.

Furthermore, when you are fatigued you have an increased amount of waste products in your system. The nerves and muscles function less efficiently because the oxygen and nutrient supply from the organs to the muscles diminishes. Also, physical fatigue often is caused by, or leads to, mental fatigue and apathy, making the body more susceptible to injury. Physical improvement cannot be enjoyed under such adverse conditions.

Maximum results in competition require maximum effort in training along with discipline in all phases of life.

PSYCHING UP

To an athlete, "psyching up" means becoming totally mentally prepared for any task that he or she embarks on. You can't rely on being physically fit; you must be mentally fit as well. If you wish to attain the goals that you have set, you must be mentally and physically prepared to push your body to its limits. To be successful at this, you have to get psyched.

Pittsburgh Steeler Mike Webster, one of the strongest men in professional football and an All-Pro, says, "Weight training is unlike other forms of conditioning. To make any real gains, you have to like lifting weights." Liking what you do is part of getting psyched, and when you see gains, you naturally want to see more gains.

In weight training, you must *always* be psyched up, not just when you go to the weightroom, but during every set, every rep, for every day, month, and year that you lift.

Motivation is a natural by-product of any plan based on realistic goals which are achievable yet challenging, and which can be achieved in a reasonable period of time—such as eleven or twelve weeks. When you leave the weightroom today you will know exactly what you will be asking of your body tomorrow. The achievement of your daily goals and the satisfaction you'll find in reaching them will result as you drive yourself to your daily physical limits—where you come close to being all you can be. There is not a man alive who cannot do more—much more—than he thinks he can.

The beautiful thing about this type of training is that you will build a degree of mental toughness which is highly prized but not commonly found among many athletes. Indeed, it carries over into aspects of maturity that are far more important than anything registered on scoreboards. Training to win is, in fact the essence of sport.

YEARLY OVERVIEW CHART

Month	Basketball Practice Schedule	Cycle Training Schedule (Strength)	Cycle Training Schedule (Conditioning)
April	No practice	4 week foundation	Distance running base
May	A—Spring off— Season workouts	4 week preparation	Interval speed work
June		3 week pre-competition (11 weeks)	Pure speed and agility work
July	B—Summer off— Season workouts	Two week between cycles—Active rest period	
Aug		4 week foundation	Distance running base
Sept		4 week preparation	Interval speed work
Oct		3 week pre-competition (11 weeks)	Pure speed and agility work
Nov	Basketball	In-Season	Coaches handle
Dec	Practice and	Maintenance	Conditioning on
Jan	Regular	Phase	Court
Feb	Season		
March		Two week active rest period at the end of season	

Ouch! A pinch from the skinfold caliper is a reasonably accurate way to quickly measure an athlete's body fat percentage.

4
DIET AND NUTRITION

Before we begin to discuss your strength training program, we must be sure that we're starting with a strong foundation; that is, a strong body. It's a pretty safe bet that if you eat badly, you're going to look and feel badly.

In order to build your body, you must feed it correctly. This chapter will show you how to do just that.

MUSCLE vs. FAT

The following principles of diet and nutrition should also be understood at the outset:

1. Any increase in body weight should be in muscle because a low-fat body leads to improved athletic performance.

2. In order to maintain, increase, or decrease body weight, it is necessary to make adjustments according to individual needs. These adjustments pertain to the ratio between calories (energy) taken in and calories (energy) burned as fuel.

3. We have learned from experience that a body fat content of below 12 percent seems to be ideal for basketball players. For youngsters of high school age and below, as well as for adult women, the count should be 4 to 5 percentage points higher (i.e., 16–17 percent).

Some basketball players may have a body fat count as low as 5 percent (Ralph Sampson's, for example, is 4½ percent); however, such a percentage is not desirable as a norm, because a certain amount of fat to pad the joints and provide insulation and lubrication between skin and muscles is vital to good health. Skinfold measurements, calculated with a skinfold caliper, and measurements of various body girths offer quick, easy, and acceptably accurate methods for ascertaining an athlete's body fat content. We recommend that these measurements be taken three times each year, at the conclusion of each 11-week cycle.

4. In order to gain one pound of muscle, it is necessary to take in 3,500 calories beyond the current normal requirement. Consuming

19

7,000 calories daily, when coupled with proper exercise, will then produce an average gain of one to two pounds of muscle per month, which is as fast as muscle should be added. This, of course, requires making an accurate estimate of the current caloric intake. For younger athletes, this may require the help of parents, the family doctor, a dietician, the local sportsmedical clinic, or a knowledgeable home economics teacher at school. If you desire to *lose* weight, the ideal amount lost per month should not exceed six to eight pounds. When medically supervised, the weight loss can be as high as fifteen pounds per month, but you must remember that too rapid a loss is almost always coupled with a corresponding loss of strength. Physical exercise should always accompany any change in caloric intake.

5. A basketball player is not a professional bodybuilder and should avoid the faddish pre-contest diets advertised in muscle magazines. Diets of this type are often extremely high in proteins and extremely low in carbohydrates and fats.

Also keep these facts in mind:

- The diet should be 55% carbohydrates, 15% protein, 30% fat.
- Carbohydrates are the energy and muscle fuels.
- Performance can be sustained 4 times longer on a high carbohydrate diet than high protein and/or increased fat diet.
- Protein is for building and repair.
- Vitamin, mineral, and protein supplements have never been shown to improve anyone's performance.
- A normal diet provides all vitamins, minerals, and protein necessary.
- You cannot perform optimally on less than 3 meals per day.
- To add weight eat light meals six times a day.
- Breakfast provides the fuel for afternoon competition.

PRE-GAME MEALS

The best pre-game meal is one that is high in carbohydrates and, therefore, easily digestible. The traditional steak meal, heavy in protein and fat content, will still be in your stomach at game time because of its poorer digestibility, this causes the blood to be diverted to the stomach instead of fueling the muscles during exercise. The pre-game meal should be eaten 3 to 5 hours before a game, and should consist mainly of carbohydrates, such as noodles, rice, cereals, or potatoes. Avoid overeating, since a feeling of fullness or bloatedness is detrimental to athletic performance. Of course, you should still eat things you like; there's no point in eating mashed potatoes if you just *hate* mashed potatoes. There are plenty of foods you can substitute. At game time, you should have plenty of fluids in your body. This will prevent you from becoming dehydrated.

WEIGHT-LOSS TIPS

At some point, many players find that they need to lose weight. Your doctor or coach can put you on a diet, and in the meantime, remember these tips.

1. Eat light P.M. meal.
2. Eat slowly.
3. Stop eating before you are full.
4. Exercising will suppress your appetite before a meal so you'll eat less. Also, get some light exercise after P.M. meal; try walking.
5. Snacks—try low calorie carrots, celery, plain popcorn, or lettuce instead of the usual junk food.
6. Prepare food in small quantities; you'll be less likely to eat as much.
7. Substitute low calorie food for high calorie, such as protein for carbohydrates, salads, vegetables for starches, fish for meat.
8. Eat low calorie desserts, for example, fruit.
9. Try to avoid situations where you tend to overeat, and avoid foods you tend to eat a lot of. This is known as behavior modification.
10. Weigh yourself each morning.

11. Drink 2 glasses of water or plain tea before meals.
12. Write down everything you eat and try to eliminate extras.
13. Cut down on salty foods, and don't *add* salt to your diet. Salt makes you retain water and can raise your blood pressure.
14. Get at least 30 minutes exercise a day.
15. A good goal is losing 1–2 pounds per week.

EATING RIGHT

Food supplements such as vitamins are not necessary as long as you have good eating habits that include nutritionally balanced meals. There are no studies which prove that additional amounts of protein, vitamins, or minerals are of any benefit to the athlete who is on a sound nutritional diet. However, when you do not meet the nutritional requirements for your body, or less calories are being consumed than necessary for the energy output required by basketball, a vitamin and mineral supplement or a balanced meal supplement such as Nutrament® or Ensure Plus® will prove helpful. Both of these supplements are well tolerated by the digestive tract, and can help you maintain body weight over a long and strenuous season. Nevertheless, it should be remembered that a supplement is no substitute for the "real" thing. The best program for you is to adopt regular eating habits with meals made up of a 55–60 percent carbohydrate content, 15–20 percent protein, and 20–30 percent fat.

Eating habits have a definite influence on weight gain or weight loss. Food should be chewed well for better digestion. Remember, it is what your body absorbs that counts, not what it consumes. Also, eat smaller amounts more often, and only when you are actually hungry. This will keep your stomach small and your midsection lean. Stop eating immediately when you start feeling full. In general, substitute fruits and other carbohydrates for sugar and sweets, and remember—you are what you eat.

NUTRITION FACTS FOR ATHLETES

Below are the basic food groups. You should eat a wide variety of foods from all four groups.

Milk & Milk Products	Fruits & Vegetables	Meats	Cereals
Milk	Citrus	Beef	Breads
Cheese	(Oranges	Pork	Oatmeal
Cottage Cheese	Grapefruits)	Fish	Macaroni
Ice Cream	Apples	Poultry	Rice
Milk Shake	Peaches	Eggs	Corn
	Potatoes	Veal	Whole grain breakfast cereals
	Pears	Lamb	Flour
	Beans	Liver	Spaghetti
	Leafy Vegetables (Spinach, Lettuce, Cabbage)		
	Tomatoes		
	Bananas		
	Carrots		

CARBOHYDRATES (CHO)		FATS		PROTEINS	
Starch	Sugar	Animal	Vegetable	Animal	Vegetable
Rice	Syrup	Meat	Nuts	Meats	Legumes
Cereals	Sugar	Eggs	Legumes	Fish	Flour
Flour	Candy	Butter	Vegetable Oil	Milk	Products
Potatoes	Fruit	Lard	Salad Dressing	Products	
Corn	Jam	Fish	Pastries	Eggs	
Noodles	Honey				
Cake					

5

FLEXIBILITY AND STRETCHING:
THE OFTEN-NEGLECTED FACTORS

"A proper warm-up is designed to increase the body's pulse rate, respiratory rate, body temperature, and range of joint mobility in order to create a condition of readiness in the athlete."
Bill Starr, The Strongest Shall Survive

Machines function most efficiently after a certain warm-up period. The human body, a "machine" infinitely more complex than any man-made device, is no different. A body that has been motionless for some time can be compared to the internal combustion engine of a car that has been sitting in front of the house throughout a cold winter night. Most modern cars have an automatic choke that assures a higher idling speed and keeps the engine from stalling. Unfortunately, the human body has no regulating mechanism that can be switched on and off, although the nervous system, under special circumstances, does provide a kind of "automatic choke" that causes an extra flow of adrenalin and almost-

instant readiness for high-speed action even from a "cold start." But this flow of adrenalin is subconsciously triggered and is not usually subject to the will. Therefore, you have to make a conscious effort to get your "machine" ready to function at a high performance level. The only way to do this from a cold start is by warming up. Unfortunately flexibility decreases with age, so good warm-up habits begun in youth will be more easily sustained in later life. Thus, a basketball player, no matter how flexible and eager to get started on a workout, should never proceed without thoroughly warming up.

WARMING UP

An effective warm-up will:

- increase blood circulation;
- increase the temperature of the muscles and blood, thereby improving oxygen assimilation;

- increase the oxygen intake, improving the recovery rate;
- reduce pulmonary blood flow resistance in the lungs, thereby improving the recovery rate between bursts of energy;
- reduce muscle viscosity, thereby reducing chances of torn or strained muscles;
- increase the speed and force of muscular contradiction, allowing a higher performance level;
- dilate the blood vessels of the skeletal muscles, again reducing the chances of injury;
- prepare certain muscle groups for coordinated functioning; and
- condition the nervous system for instantaneous reactions.

A warmed-up muscle will be a more efficient muscle, and a warmed-up body will always be a better-protected body and a better-functioning mechanism under the stress of exercise. At the Universtity of Virginia, we call our warm-up period "prelims," short for pre-practice preliminaries. The duration of this warm-up period varies according to the needs of the day, but under no circumstances is it under 10 minutes, and usually it lasts 15 to 18 minutes.

As the strength training and conditioning program for basketball at Virginia has been developed, a variety of different in-season warm-up exercises have been used effectively. Among them are:

- light jogging around the gymnasium perimeter for about five minutes, followed by shooting foul shots for six to eight minutes;
- various light calisthenics such as toe touching, side straddle hops (jumping jacks), arm rotation, side bends, etc. (10–12 minutes);
- light form running drills for ten to twelve minutes;
- taking shots from around the basket, both standing and jumping, all the while concentrating on optimal shooting technique with each shot. Distance from the basket is increased until maximum range with accuracy is reached (about 15 minutes).

During the off-season, warm-ups involve no running or shooting drills, but the period of stretching movements is lengthened.

FLEXIBILITY

You probably know at least one individual who is immensely strong but so limited in range of motion that his or her strength cannot be used to any advantage. It is vital, then, that basketball players strive for the greatest range of mobility possible. The difference between some flexibility and a lot of flexibility might just provide the margin between victory and defeat.

To gear the flexibility program to individual needs is very important, and while it takes effort, the rewards justify that effort. You must completely turn your thoughts inward and eliminate any competition with teammates. The competition is with yourself, comparing your ability to the ability you had at your last workout. Concentrating on yourself is going to increase your ability to "feel" your body, to "listen" to it and hear what it is trying to say. To develop a "feeling" for your own body is very important because tension, muscle tightness, and fatigue levels vary from day to day and make daily adjustments necessary. Here are the most obvious reasons for maintaining good flexibility.

1. increased range of motion;
2. relaxed muscle attachments;
3. relaxed joint tissues;
4. improved coordination;
5. more efficient movement;
6. decrease in, or elimination of, common strains resulting from muscle tightness (groin, calf, hamstrings, quadriceps, and lower back);
7. increased strength in extreme motion ranges resulting in increased on-court effectiveness;
8. reduction of other injuries, especially

those resulting from fast starts and extensive striding.

Some reasons for poor flexibility are:

1. decrease in muscle size resulting from insufficient activity;
2. shortened muscles, also due to lack of exercise;
3. excess fat around the joints;
4. limited range of motion when performing exercises.

The most obvious reason for lack of flexibility, however, is usually a lack of willpower and dedication on an athlete's part. Do not fall into the trap of considering flexibility exercises a waste of time that keep you from getting on with the really "important" part of the workout!

PNF STRETCHING

Most coaches and athletes are familiar with self-imposed static stretching, which is a fine way to loosen muscle attachments and tighten joint tissues. Here, however, we are presenting a more efficient way that builds strength as well as range of motion in the most extreme leverage positions, a fact that is vitally important in improving basketball performance.

The flexibility concepts of PNF stretching (or *Proprioceptive Neuromuscular Facilitation*) will work for every joint and can be performed by athletes under an instructor's direction, or on their own time. Approximately 15 minutes of PNF stretching can result in hair-trigger readiness to commence all workouts.

What PNF stretching actually does is to make the functioning of the nerves, muscles, and the Golgi tendon organ (the organ which causes the muscles to shut down under extreme stress) much easier.

Basketball players often encounter extreme stress that must be overcome (lifting a weight, moving an opponent, propelling an object or one's body through the air). It is often out of necessity that such stress must

be overcome from an extreme or unusual position.

Repeated effort and concentration on PNF stretching will allow you not only to assume extreme positions at will, but also to exert great force in those positions. These exercises will not only improve the strength of the connective tissues of the tendons but also will improve the strength of the attachments of the tendons to the bones.

The PNF Stretching Method

These stretches, also called "hold-relax," are done by creating resistance, holding the position, and then relaxing the muscle for a few moments. You can do these stretches by yourself or with a partner who can create resistance for you.

Always remember that you should never push yourself too hard. There are those who say, "No pain, no gain," but that's not true when it comes to stretching. Over-doing it can lead to pulled muscles, and *that* leads to time on the bench!

COOL-DOWN

Just as it is important to warm-up prior to strenuous exercise, so is it important to give the body a chance to "calm down" afterward; to cool off, although not too rapidly. To use an earlier analogy, a car that has been driven on the highway for a prolonged period of time, at high speed, should not have its engine turned off immediately upon pulling into a rest stop, gas station, or garage; rather, the engine should be allowed to idle for a few minutes to find an output level appropriate for the "rest period." The human body, too, after a period of high-level activity, should be allowed to find its "normal" cadence without going from a state of high activity to one of nonactivity.

Usually, a period of eight to ten minutes is enough to allow the blood that has been pumped into the muscles to return from the extremities to the major organs. This period should be filled with slow-moving, rhythmic activities such as the following:

- PNF stretching/abdominal hangs
- Light jogging
- Walking
- Swimming
- A combination of any of the above

The foundation of a super workout: Ralph Sampson and friends demonstrate important stretches. Pictured here (clockwise from top left) are the single leg hamstring, the hamstring and back stretch, and the pectoral stretch.

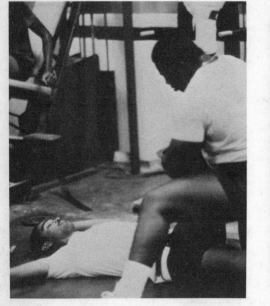

Stretching regularly not only enhances an athlete's flexibility, it also decreases the likelihood of injury. Pictured here are some stretches for the upper body (clockwise from top): shoulder and lat stretch, groin stretch, and shoulder and arm stretch.

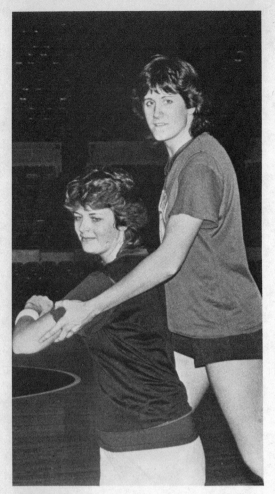

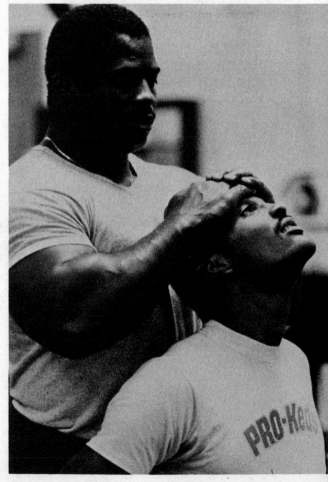

Clockwise from top: trunk rotation, deltoid and shoulder stretch, backward neck stretch, and shoulder and arm stretch.

Opposite page, (clockwise from top left): Sampson performs a full set of neck stretches. In each case Sampson uses his neck muscles to create resistance.

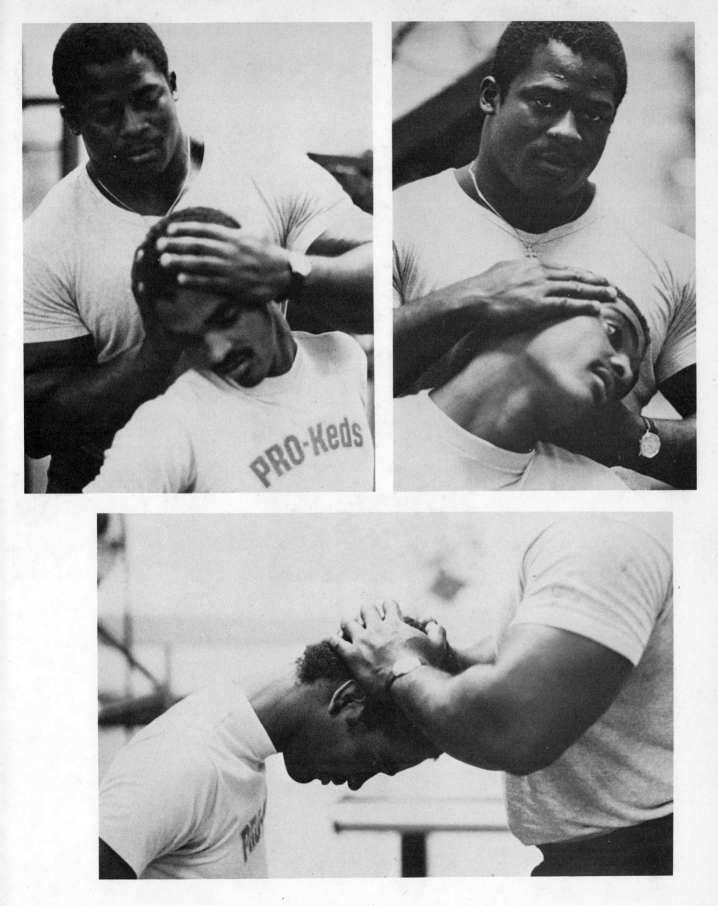

Huge! Ralph Sampson works his biceps doing cable curls on a cable crossover machine.

6

SELECTING A TRAINING SYSTEM

You've determined that you need to have a training system. Now the question is, *how* do you select a system that's right for you?

To select the best program, three important factors must be addressed. The first is that your specific needs have to be met. The second is the problem of so many conflicting training theories. And the third, already discussed, is that the solution must take into consideration both of the above points as well as the type of equipment and the amount of space available for training in each individual program. Let's look at these points in order.

THE NEEDS OF AN ATHLETE

A comprehensive system of strength training and conditioning must cover five basic principles if you are to receive the maximum benefit. These points are:

1. Frequency (how often to train);
2. Duration (how long to train);
3. Intensity (how much work);
4. Variation (which exercises); and most important,
5. Specificity (direct application to basketball).

SO MANY PROGRAMS TO CHOOSE FROM

During the past twenty years there has been an abundance of conflicting theories regarding strength training for specific sports, particularly football and basketball. In general, these conflicts are as follows:

A. What speed should a basketball player train at (explosive vs. nonexplosive work)?

B. Should free weights, machines, or a combination be used?

C. Finally, how many sets and repetitions should be performed for best results? (For example, the Nautilus concept of one or two sets that push your body to its limits as opposed to the various multiset and repetition theories.)

31

The primary question that coaches, parents, and athletes must answer is which system of training will give you the winning edge as you perform on the court.

THE SOLUTION: CYCLE TRAINING

The first step in reaching a solution is to realize that athletes cannot allow themselves to become out of shape in the off-season. In other words, year-round training is a necessity.

The program we recommend is the system we teach at the University of Virginia, called "Periodization" or "Cycle-Training," which is simply a form of long-range planning. This training system was developed by sports scientists in the Soviet Union to assist promising young athletes in meeting specific needs. By using long-range planning, athletes can be trained (or train themselves) to their individual physical and mental peaks for those times they need to be at the top of their form, and at the same time they can learn to avoid the rampant problems of overtraining and premature peaking.

Each year should be broken up (as indicated in the Yearly Overview Chart in Chapter 2) into several specific blocks of time, with the ultimate long-range goal being to develop athletes that are mentally and physically superior to the opponents they will meet during the coming season.

The second step in developing a comprehensive training system for basketball is to realize that you cannot be brought to a strength and conditioning peak effectively more than twice per year. Why? Because if the frequency, duration, and intensity of training is too great or continues for too long, you will become fatigued. This will, in most cases, result in the program becoming boring and monotonous, causing the central nervous system simply to shut down without further physical gains. The most effective way to avoid this discouraging situation is to have sharp breaks in training (in terms of sets, reps, and exercises) at regular intervals, thus spurring the nervous system to renewed growth. The major advantage of "periodization" is that, better than any other known system of training, it takes the five major components of basketball strength/power training into consideration. Furthermore, it does this in such a way as to drastically reduce the potential danger of overtraining while providing the greatest possible opportunity for continuous improvement.

Experience and research has shown that training equipment used for one or two sets to momentary failure cannot bring about optimal conditioning for the sport of basketball. Multiple set and repetition training is crucial to continuing progress.

In addition, varying speeds of training, and a wide variety of equipment can and should be utilized as well. Even if you're working within a limited budget or you have limited access to equipment, you should not fall for the myth that outstanding physical development cannot be achieved without some specific product or any one company's equipment. As we mentioned in Chapter 2, this simply is not true.

We advocate using a wide variety of both equipment and exercises and, at this point, we recommend that a combination of free weights and machines be used.

One other point regarding explosive vs. nonexplosive speed of training is that great balance (body control) is vital to playing basketball well. Athletes must strive to develop strength and flexibility, with balance, in extreme motion ranges. To this end, exercises should always be performed in a strict, controlled manner, never allowing the resistance to "free-fall." During the forward range of motion, or the completion of the lift to lockout, you should always drive the resistance upward with the most explosive possible effort on all repetitions.

Let us now look at this remarkable training system.

Cycle Training Explained

The length of the competitive basketball season naturally varies with the level of play. However, four and one-half to five months is generally the average. By looking again at the Yearly Overview Chart, it becomes apparent that two strength/conditioning cycles of approximately 11 weeks each will fit in just right so that you'll be completely prepared for the upcoming season. An active rest period of 10–14 days should separate these cycles, and there should be a 10-day, two week break from all training at each season's end. Never omit these intervals of both mental and physical recuperation, as they are extremely important to your long-term progress.

The periods of both strength training and conditioning can be broken into four parts: foundation, preparation, pre-competition and in-season maintenance. The specifics of each phase will be covered in Chapters 7 and 9, but for clarification purposes we will highlight the basic principles here.

The Four-Week Foundation

The four-week foundation period is when the physical base is established. This phase stresses lower intensity (high repetitions) and higher volume in terms of exercise. This is the time during which maximum strength is improved, an endurance base is built (both muscular and cardiovascular), injuries are rehabilitated, and any weaknesses or imbalances are discovered through testing and are positively altered.

All sets during this phase should be performed for ten repetitions, with gradually increasing poundages.

This early training will prepare you for high-quality and high-intensity strength and power training. In addition, by decreasing body fat content and increasing muscle mass, your potential for gains across the board is improved.

The conditioning base is established during this phase by distance running on alternate days. Training in this way will result not only in positive body composition change, but also in the improved potential for strength and conditioning during the remaining weeks of each cycle, as well as a marked improvement in short-term endurance.

The Preparation Period

In the preparation period (four weeks long) the intensity increases to a medium level. Effort is always maximum, but, repetitions and poundages are decreased to fives with significant weight increases. Strength and power must be emphasized during this phase as well, although you should still be striving to develop your entire body by improving all physical qualities. The volume of exercises performed is still quite high. This basic strength training will further build up the fitness base so that power specialization and even higher-intensity work can be performed later.

Overall strength, and particularly lower-extremity strength, will dramatically improve during this phase.

Here again, the conditioning base is further developed by moving away from long-distance running in favor of interval sprints and agilities. In addition, hopping and bounding drills (plyometrics) and various depth jumps will have been gradually worked on as well, and the interval and speed training will become very high quality.

The Pre-Competition Period

In the pre-competition period you are brought to a peak in both strength and conditioning. This period will last approximately three weeks, and is the time of high intensity work with all activities becoming very sport-specific. That is, assistant exercises are reduced, the lifting poundages are increased again, and the repetitions are cut to three on all exercises, with maximum speed and agility work being performed.

This third stage is the payoff period, and in every case we have encountered, tremendous increases in power have occurred here. At this point, you should be "maxed-out" (tested) on all lifts.

Record your best times on all conditioning drills and speed work. We are confident that the results and the accompanying sense of accomplishment will excite both you and your coach.

Remember that this is the point at which either basketball practice begins or a short rest is taken before the beginning of the second cycle (which will lead into the competitive season).

In-Season Maintenance

The final phase is in-season maintenance and it is always followed by a two-week rest period.

At this time the major emphasis is on the sport itself. Conditioning is handled by the basketball coaches, and strength training is cut down in order to ensure that enough quality work is performed to maintain the level previously achieved, while not tapping into energy levels needed to play basketball. Repetitions during this stage will vary according to needs.

CHARTING YOUR PROGRESS

Progress should be charted by keeping appropriate workout logs. Pertinent information can be recorded by the coach, trainer, team manager, parent, or by yourself. This should be adhered to year-round, both in and out of season.

Among the points to be listed are the following:

1. Agility times
2. Interval 220-yard sprint times
3. Body weight versus body fat content
4. Vertical jump (and reach) improvements
5. Starting points and goals
6. Sets and repetitions of all exercises
7. Poundage lifted, especially the day's goal, which is always the top set

Also, rehabilitation routines should be recorded whenever you are sick or injured and unable to perform the prescribed lifting or conditioning program for that day. This routine should be worked out and established in consultation with a trainer, team physician, or family doctor.

Keep your daily log in a notebook, along with a written statement of your personal goals.

In addition, starting at the outset of each cycle and periodically (quarterly) thereafter, have a snapshot taken of yourself to put in the notebook. As the saying goes, one picture is worth a thousand words; when the first results of the strength and conditioning training become apparent, comparison of the pictures provides a tremendous motivational tool.

In the Appendix, you'll find examples of workout logs. You can design your own logs with the help of your coach, or feel free to use these.

GO FOR IT!

This explanation of periodization is simply a guideline for comprehensive basketball training. The key point is starting with a general type of exercise and lower intensity, then progressing to higher and higher intensities the more advanced the player becomes. The sharp changes in volume and intensity will shock the central nervous system and cause a stronger and increasingly positive adaptive response from each athlete's body.

Finally, remember that the major goal in strength training as well as conditioning is to develop yourself until you are mentally and physically superior to the opponents you will. meet in the upcoming season. Fully implemented, this training system will ensure that this goal is reached.

CYCLE TRAINING OUTLINE

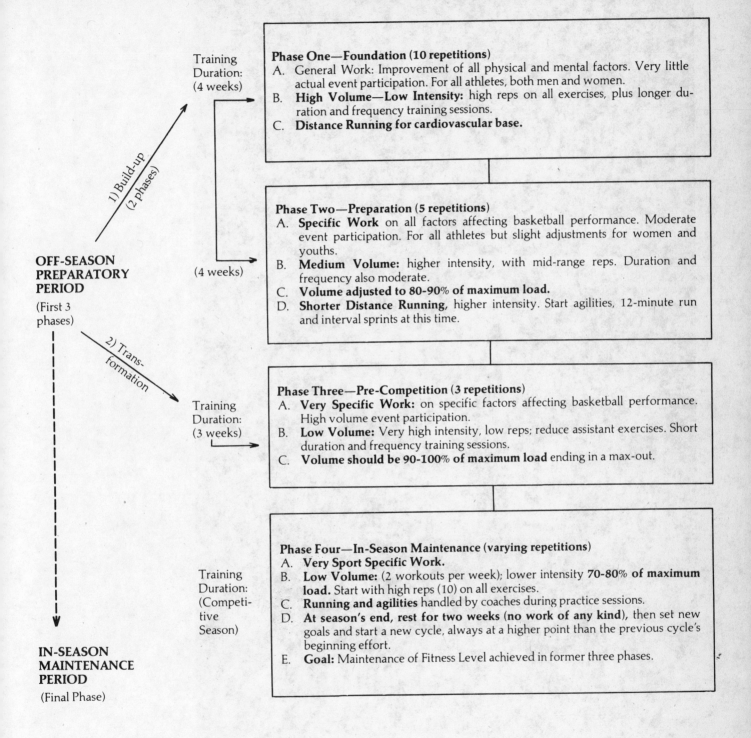

Training Duration:
(4 weeks)

Phase One—Foundation (10 repetitions)
A. General Work: Improvement of all physical and mental factors. Very little actual event participation. For all athletes, both men and women.
B. **High Volume—Low Intensity:** high reps on all exercises, plus longer duration and frequency training sessions.
C. **Distance Running for cardiovascular base.**

1) Build-up (2 phases)

OFF-SEASON PREPARATORY PERIOD

(First 3 phases)

(4 weeks)

Phase Two—Preparation (5 repetitions)
A. **Specific Work** on all factors affecting basketball performance. Moderate event participation. For all athletes but slight adjustments for women and youths.
B. **Medium Volume:** higher intensity, with mid-range reps. Duration and frequency also moderate.
C. **Volume adjusted to 80-90% of maximum load.**
D. **Shorter Distance Running,** higher intensity. Start agilities, 12-minute run and interval sprints at this time.

2) Trans-formation

Training Duration:
(3 weeks)

Phase Three—Pre-Competition (3 repetitions)
A. **Very Specific Work:** on specific factors affecting basketball performance. High volume event participation.
B. **Low Volume:** Very high intensity, low reps; reduce assistant exercises. Short duration and frequency training sessions.
C. **Volume should be 90-100% of maximum load** ending in a max-out.

IN-SEASON MAINTENANCE PERIOD

(Final Phase)

Training Duration:
(Competitive Season)

Phase Four—In-Season Maintenance (varying repetitions)
A. **Very Sport Specific Work.**
B. **Low Volume:** (2 workouts per week); lower intensity **70-80% of maximum load.** Start with high reps (10) on all exercises.
C. **Running and agilities** handled by coaches during practice sessions.
D. **At season's end, rest for two weeks (no work of any kind),** then set new goals and start a new cycle, always at a higher point than the previous cycle's beginning effort.
E. **Goal:** Maintenance of Fitness Level achieved in former three phases.

7
STRENGTH IMPROVEMENT

Your training cycle may now begin with the deep-seated confidence which comes only to those who have adequately prepared.

Cycle training is an excellent choice for a training system. Why? Because, when properly understood and fully implemented, this method guarantees "big time" results.

We firmly believe that this system will dramatically improve your basketball performance. Creating physical and mental attributes which will convert quickly and directly to the development of basketball skills is the bottom line.

Regardless of the level of skill you have currently attained, you are now ready to meet the training challenge. The material in the last six chapters, covering the first two weeks of preparation, has seen to that.

The next workout will begin the first phase of your cycle. We encourage you to look upon us as your strength and conditioning coaches. We will guide you just as if we were face to face, and will help you turn hopes and dreams into accomplishments. Regardless of who or where you are, more can be achieved than you ever imagined possible.

MAKING THE TRAINING SYSTEM WORK FOR YOU

Basketball players, particularly those at advanced levels of play, now, more than ever, believe that developing the qualities needed to play basketball cannot be accomplished simply by playing the game itself.

One thing is for sure: regardless of which system of training you use, the results must translate into improved basketball performance. This is the bottom line of all training programs.

If you are to be challenged and motivated, you must be convinced that hard work in this training program will enable you to shoot more accurately and from longer range, jump higher (and quicker), endure longer, run faster, and possess more quickness and agility—in short, to play better basketball.

In order to induce maximum results from training, your mind must first be strong. Then, and only then, will your body adapt to workout stress in the desired manner. You must develop a "heart to train," in order to push yourself to your limits. Because of the significance of this need, we try to constantly reinforce the following points:

- No two athletes respond in exactly the same manner, so do not try to be just like someone else. You must find out for yourself what your body is saying and react accordingly, not just sometimes or in some things, but all the time, and in all training. Seek to "fine tune" yourself to a hair-trigger readiness to compete, while you work to complement other members of the team as well.
- You must continue to achieve your daily training goals, for it is these "little victories" that ultimately produce champions. These daily objectives must be challenging but within reach because nothing breeds success like success. Above all, don't hesitate to pat yourself on the back when you've done well.
- Be supportive of your teammates. They'll appreciate it, and they'll return the favor. Above all, be enthusiastic. It's contagious.

As we mentioned earlier, great strength alone does not guarantee the ability to perform a specialized game of skill such as basketball. Capability to develop your skill, however, cannot exist unless you possess considerable strength. In other words, strength does not guarantee skill, but in order to execute basketball skills well, you must have strength. Coupling strength with the other physical attributes and with skill is the answer. Basketball players, although normally tall and lanky, need not be—and indeed must not be—weak.

THE WOMAN ATHLETE

Athletes are athletes, regardless of whether they are male or female. However, when it comes to weight training there *are* some differences that you should be aware of.

There is no doubt that women can compete in a strenuous athletic activity and attain a high level of physical performance without sustaining physiological or psychological damage. Because of misconceptions, stereotyped thinking, and social custom, women for many years were not allowed to participate at the high level of athletic competition enjoyed by their male counterparts. Even in terms of relative levels of strength and performance they were relegated to a weaker, physically inferior role.

While it is not the purpose of this book to delve into conditioning for all women's sports, regarding basketball we will make the following observations:

- The female basketball player may initially experience a slight increase in body weight due to the increase in muscle mass. This increase in bodyweight is temporary.
- In some instances, she may experience a small decrease in muscular strength the day immediately preceeding menstruation. Once again, this is temporary.
- Strength training for women in basketball will not cause excessive muscle tissue. Even though muscular strength increases, strength training does not result in muscle bulk due to the low level of the hormone testosterone in the female.

Although female hormones have a growth-inhibiting effect, women's muscles, like those of men, develop in an overload state.

Another factor contributing to the lack of muscular development in women is the higher ratio of fat tissue to muscle mass. This ten percent or so of additional adipose (fat) tissue tends to obscure the visual definition of developed muscle in the female.

Thus, the female basketball player will experience little or no increase in total body weight due to strength training, but will rather experience a decrease in body fat and an increase in lean muscle size.

We are often asked questions about strength and conditioning programs for women. The most commonly asked questions—and our answers—are:

What are some of the benefits women will derive from a sound strength and conditioning program?

First, a measurable loss of fat tissue. Systematic exercise along with proper diet and strength training/conditioning will improve the female figure by streamlining muscles and improving tone. Plus, increased strength will be accompanied by better muscular control and coordination. Furthermore, because strength training places stress on the muscle tendon units as well as the connective tissues, injuries become less likely. The added stress on the connective tissues leads to a greater contractibility. Thus, strength increases and muscular strains and joint looseness decrease.

Will strength training slow the female basketball player down and make her less flexible?

NO! In fact, the opposite will occur since a sound program builds muscles and endurance in normally neglected areas of the female body. Furthermore, where momentum and power are taken in combination with strength and flexibility work, and, since velocity is held constant and power is increased by improving the force production, improvement in foot speed will result.

Should strength training programs designed for women be different from those of men?

Strength gains in female have been equal to or better than those in men. One reason has been identified as the lower initial strength levels of many women. Regardless of the reason, women are capable of making enormous strength gains.

Basically, training programs for female basketball players need not differ drastically from those of males regarding training frequency (how often), duration (length of cycle), and intensity (work and overload). But, just as with men, the amount of weight handled must be manageable. If necessary, start with the bar and no weight. Weight increases of 2½ pounds rather than the usual 5 or 10 for men, are common for females—particularly beginners.

Constant improvements in all of the areas previously mentioned continue to excite us and encourage our efforts with female basketball players. It has been exciting and challenging for us to play a small role in the emergence of strength and conditioning programs for women.

The bottom line is this: there is *nothing* feminine about weakness.

BASIC PRINCIPLES

The following 15 guidelines are extremely important.

1. Your off-season workouts will take about 1½ hours per training session to complete, including warm-up and stretching. This time must be maximized, so beginning immediately you must mentally discipline yourself to concentrate totally for the entire duration of each and every workout. This is vital.

2. During the first 4-week cycle (foundation phase) train in the weightroom four times per week. In the 4-week preparation and 3-week pre-competition phases, workouts will be three times per week. The in-season maintenance phase will cover the entire competitive season and will require two weightroom workouts per week.

3. Never work out alone with free weights. Ideally, three players should train together, so that when one is performing an exercise, the other two can spot and load.

4. Always wear a lifting belt, as the added support will help in completing all lifts. These belts should fit snugly but not tightly. They will also help keep the important lower back area warm. A lifting belt can be purchased at most sporting goods stores.

5. Wrap your knees for the top two sets of squats. These wraps should be durable but soft. When applying these supports, be sure to keep your legs straight and crisscross the wrap around the knee. Do not wrap straight around as this will create a tendency to slip and restrict blood circulation. Crisscrossing, on the other hand, will lock the support in place and not hamper blood flow.

Wrist straps are another helpful item (obtainable in the same manner). An old military belt or car seat belt about ten inches in length will also serve the purpose.

Also, regular gymnast's chalk (magnesium carbonate) will improve your grip by helping absorb palm sweat. Most sporting goods distributors and drugstores carry it.

6. Basketball requires both cardiovascular

and muscular endurance, so do not take more than 2½–3 minutes rest between sets and exercises, particularly during the initial foundation phase when the physical base for the season is being established.

7. Train with poundages that you can comfortably handle for all sets and repetitions. This point is vital to long-term progress.

8. The primary sources of strength in your body are the thigh, hip, and buttock muscles. The further you get away from this area when training, the less potential exists for appropriate strength development. For example, on all vertical pulling exercises, such as power cleans, if the bar gets out in front of your torso more than four or five inches, it doubles the pressure on the lower back, instantly causing you to be handling twice the poundage actually on the bar. For this reason, every repetition in every set and exercise must be performed in the strictest possible fashion.

9. Never "cheat" to lift more weight. Cheating often brings other muscles into play, which lessens the effectiveness of the movement being performed, and often leads to overtraining and even injury.

10. Perform all exercises from full extension to maximum contraction, as this practice will develop strength and promote increased flexibility throughout the muscles' entire length.

11. Begin after warm-up with the most difficult part of the day's training load. Work out the major muscle groups of the chest, legs, or back first.

12. Proper breathing is very important. When doing leg, chest, and abdominal exercises, you should start to exhale at the point of greatest stress. For example, in the bench press exercise, inhale (mouth open) deeply as the resistance is taken from the spotter at lift-off, and exhale as you drive the weight back to the starting position. In most cases, normal breathing will be fine when exercising the arms, shoulders, and back.

13. Perform all exercises in a slow and controlled manner; then, at the exact point and moment of contact, drive hard toward the completion "lock-out" position.

In order for muscles to become larger and/or stronger, they must be taxed (overloaded). This may be accomplished in numerous ways, among which are:

- Increasing the repetitions
- Increasing the repititions
- Doing more work
- Decreasing the rest interval between sets and exercises

14. After working to develop strength and power, do not make the all-too-common mistake of assuming you are strong enough to play and then abruptly discontinue workouts. Strength must be maintained, and discontinuing workouts will leave you vulnerable to injuries, since the joints become less stable as the muscles decrease in size due to lack of work. Even a relatively short period of inactivity (over four days) can produce a substantial deterioration in both cardiovascular and muscular endurance, as well as in strength, flexibility, muscular body weight, and, as a consequence, skill.

15. Remember, overtraining is a common occurrence even among the most experienced athletes. Unless adequate recovery time and proper diet are parts of the strength and conditioning equation, no significant gains will be achieved. Gains occur during the rest/recovery periods between workouts. In other words, you do not get stronger while you train, but while you recover from training. Remember this fact the next time you are tempted to skip a meal, particularly breakfast, or to eat a candy bar instead of fruit.

WEIGHT TRAINING FOR BASKETBALL

When you're working with weights, it's important that you use them correctly in order to avoid injury. Your coach or trainer can show you proper techniques, but for now, we'll show you how to weight train with exercises that are certain to help your game.

Total concentration is etched on the faces of Ralph and his spotters as he does incline dumbbell presses, great for the pectoral muscles. Notice the attention the spotters pay to make sure that the exercise is done correctly and safely.

Major Basketball Exercises

The major exercises for basketball players—men, women, and youngsters—in each cycle phase are:

- Bench press
- Parallel squats
- Power cleans or high pulls
- Incline dumbbell press (occasionally standing)

These should always be performed for five sets, but of varying repetitions (either tens, fives, or threes), depending on which cycle phase—(1) foundation, (2) preparation, (3) pre-competition, or (4) in-season maintenance—you are engaged in.

Supplementary Exercises

These exercises, usually referred to as assistants, are designed to "tie together" the major muscles involved in the four primary exercises. That is, they assist in the development of the coordinated total body strength necessary for improving basketball skills. In no particular order, as athletes have varying needs (strength and weakness areas), these supplementary exercises are:

Upper Body

- Front deltoid raises
- Various curls particularly "hammer curls"
- Pulldowns, behind the neck/to chest
- Seated rows (cable)
- Dumbbell rows
- Concentration rows
- Triceps pushes
- Tricep pushdowns
- Dips and chins
- Flys

Lower Body

- Hip sled (can be substituted for squats during the competitive season)
- Leg press
- Leg curl
- Knee extension
- Calf machine (toe raises)

How to Perform the Major Basketball Exercises

Bench Press

Lie in a supine position on a flat bench with the legs out to the side and with feet as far underneath as possible, keeping them flat on the floor and never raising the buttocks off the bench.

Using back or leg muscles reduces the benefit of the bench press. Notice that the back is kept flat on the bench, the feet are kept under the athlete, and the spotter carefully monitors the athlete's performance.

The bench press has been called "the squat of the upper body." It stresses the pectorals, deltoids, and triceps. Note that the bar is held directly over the chest at the beginning of the exercise.

Keep the head in contact with the bench. Take a chest position that is as high as possible and always take the hand off at full arm length directly above the chest. Ease the bar down very slowly, with complete control, to just below the nipple area. Pause momentarily but never relax. Then drive the weight hard off the chest, up and back until it stops directly over the bridge of the nose.

Take a deep breath, keeping the mouth open in order to equalize pressure in the chest cavity and hold it until the bar passes the point of greatest resistance, about 6 inches off the chest. Then exhale slowly and lock the lift out explosively.

Proper form is essential for the bench press. Arms are kept perpendicular to the ground throughout the exercise.

The grip should always be "overhand" with the wrists directly above the elbows at the bottom position. Hold the bar low in the palms of the hands.

Parallel Squats

The squat is unquestionably the best exercise for adding muscular strength in the legs and lower body. In addition, this exercise stimulates muscular growth throughout the entire body. Start with feet shoulder-width apart with toes pointing slightly outward, which will rotate the hips closer to the bar. Keep the head pointed upward and arch the lower back. Go down slowly to a parallel posi-

The squat is one of the most important exercises for building leg strength. At the start of the exercise, rest the bar on the trapezius muscles, not on your vertabrae. Wrap a towel around the bar if you feel any pain. Notice that the user wears a weight belt and knee bandages for support.

Raise the bar slowly, concentrating on keeping the back straight.

Lower the bar slowly until the thighs are parallel to the ground. Notice that the user's toes point slightly outwards throughout the movement.

Complete the movement, making sure to use the leg and not the back muscles. This will develop the leg muscles and prevent back injury.

tion, pause momentarily, and then explode upward. Never relax, stay tight. Breathe deeply at the starting position, exhale as you pass the point of greatest resistance, coming out of the hole (bottom). The bar should be carried low on the traps (approximately two inches below the top of the shoulder). While looking straight ahead, be sure to keep the line of vertebrae straight; then, as you come out of the bottom position, simultaneously thrust the head back and the hips forward. Work at learning to "sit" into the lift, with knees over the ankles. When performed properly (as described) squats will not adversely affect the knees, as long as you do not "free fall" with the weight or try to bounce out of the bottom.

Hip Sled

Start on your back with head and shoulders comfortably placed on the hip sled board. Place the feet at the desired width on the foot rest (about 16 inches apart). Make sure the locking mechanism is engaged by moving the lever in.

To adjust the board forward, simply grasp the hip sled hand grips and pull the board forward. Each adjustment is 2 inches. Position the hands on the hip sled board hand grips. Now inhale deeply, keeping the mouth open, and drive the weight upward to lockout. Exhale, ease the weight down, (do not relax), and repeat.

The hip sled helps build the quadriceps (the muscles on top of the thigh). At the start of the leg press, inhale deeply and, keeping your mouth open, slowly drive the weight upward.

Once the legs are fully extended, exhale and slowly lower the weight to the starting position.

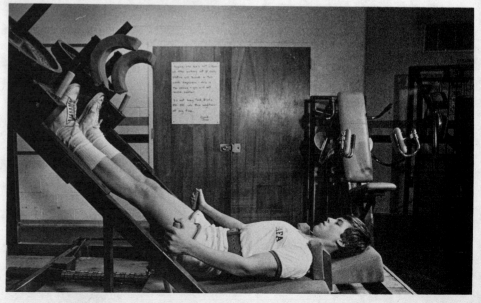

Power Clean

Take an "overhand grip" slightly wider than shoulder width, with feet flat and with a shoulder-width stance, and the bar lined up over the balls of the feet. Start the lift by extending the legs, keeping the arms fully extended. Do not jerk the bar off the floor, but push the floor away from the bar until the bar passes the knees. Be sure to keep the shoulders out in front of the bar, knees slightly bent. Again, the back must be straight. This is the pulling position.

From knee level, begin the pull by keeping the bar in close to the body. Then, just as in the squat, fully extend, right up on the toes. Simultaneously, with elbows high, shrug the shoulders and thrust the hips and elbows forward. You should feel as if you are jumping with the bar straight upward. Rack the bar on the chest by whipping the elbows under the bar upward and out.

High Pull

This is an ideal movement when slow progress is being made on power cleans, wrist trouble crops up, or excessive "cleaning" poundages force undue "lay-back" of the upper torso.

Gripping chalk and wrist wraps should be used, since this lift involves a snapping movement. The movement is performed exactly like the power clean, except that the weight is not racked on the chest. Pull as high as possible and then return to the starting position. Remember, keep the bar close to the body.

The movement relieves stress on the wrists and lower back. Be sure not to move more slowly at the top of the movement. This will defeat the purpose. Keep it snappy and explosive.

Nautilus Knee Extension

Sit on or in the machine. Taking a firm grip on the handles, inhale deeply, and extend the knee explosively to full extension. Hold mo-

The power clean is a terrific exercise because it develops explosive drive and coordination between different muscle groups. At the same time, however, it is a difficult exercise to perform correctly. Power cleans should never be done without the assistance of someone experienced with the exercise and without first practicing the correct form with light weights.

At the start of the exercise, grasp the bar so that the hands are a few inches wider than a shoulder length apart. Keeping your back slightly arched and your head level, hold the bar with your arms relaxed but fully extended. Your knees should be bent and your shoulders should be over the bar before you begin the exercise.

Start the lift by driving the legs, keeping the arms fully extended. Do not jerk the bar off the floor; push the floor away from the bar until the bar passes the knees.

After the bar passes the knees, begin the pull by keeping the bar close to the body. Then fully extend right up on the toes.

Complete the lift by whipping the elbows under the bar upward and out. This excellent exercise, if done properly, develops the trapezius muscles and strengthens the lower back.

The high pull is an good way to supplement power cleans. It develops the entire girdle of shoulder muscles. The motion of this exercise is the same as in cleans, but begins from a standing position with the bar hanging at an arm's length.

While extending, and keeping the elbows high, shrug the shoulders and thrust the hips and elbows forward.

mentarily; exhale slowly as the poundage is lowered in a controlled manner to the starting position. Inhale and repeat.

Nautilus Leg Curl

Lie flat on the machine, grip the appropriate side handles, place the padded roller bar near the heel and, while keeping the hips down, pull upward to the buttocks. Hold for a moment, lower slowly without any jerking and with good control, and repeat. Inhale at the beginning and exhale as the repetition is completed.

Nautilus Pullover

Always keep the chest high as this is a deep-breathing exercise. Exhale deeply and grip the bars approximately twenty inches apart. Lower in a semi-circle movement past the head and chest all the way down to the lower abdomen and return, exhaling on the way back. Use a deep-breathing, controlled movement.

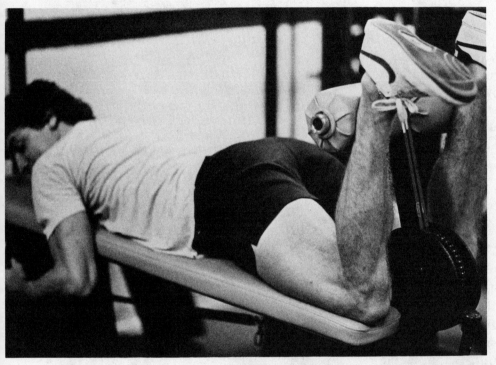

Leg curls develop the muscles of the back of the leg (the hamstrings) without stressing the other muscles. For maximum benefit, pause a few seconds at the finishing position shown here.

Grunt! This athlete's effort is reflected on his face as he does double shoulder exercises on a Nautilus machine. This exercise works the deltoid muscles but, unlike those using barbells, allows the trainee to use more weight by concentrating the resistance on the upper arms and elbows.

Nautilus Double Shoulder

This exercise works the major muscles of the chest as well as the deltoid muscles of the shoulders. Adjust the seat until shoulders, when elbows are together, are directly under the axis of overhead cams. Fasten the belt. Place forearm behind and firmly against movement arm pads. Grasp handles tightly, thumbs around the handle, head against seat. Inhale and push the elbows together in front of the chest. Pause briefly, but do not relax. Lower the resistance slowly and repeat. Exhale on the return to the starting position.

Concentration Row

Place head on a bench with feet about 18 inches apart. Secure a grip (overhand) on the barbell that keeps the elbows directly above the wrists when the pull starts. This is a great lat (back) exercise. Keep the legs slightly bent and the back nearly parallel to the floor. Inhale deeply while pulling the bar directly to the lowest part of the chest. Do not let it touch the floor at any time. Exhale when you reach the starting position, and repeat.

Dumbbell Row

Place a dumbbell on the floor in front of the rack or bench. Place one leg forward with knee bent, the other one back and locked out. Always use a "palms-in" grip. Lift the dumbbell off the floor. Inhale and, while keeping the arm in close, pull the dumbbell straight up. Return to starting position and exhale. Squeeze your back muscles together as you work. Concentrate on the back, not on the arm pump.

Seated Row

Sit on the floor or on a very short bench or block, in front of the pulley, with pulley at about chest level. Place the feet against the front of the machine in a way that will enable you to support the weight stacks with both arms as you take hold on the handle while seated in this bent forward position. Maintain this body position throughout. Bend either

Incredible is the only way to describe the poundage pro football star Pat Chester is using to do these concentration rows. These are great for lats. Knees are kept slightly bent throughout the exercise.

Dumbbell bent rowing is another way to develop strong lats. Notice that the right leg is kept about two and a half feet behind the left. Shown here is the finish of a dumbbell bent row.

Dumbbell bent row's starting position. Notice that the arm is kept directly below the shoulder joint.

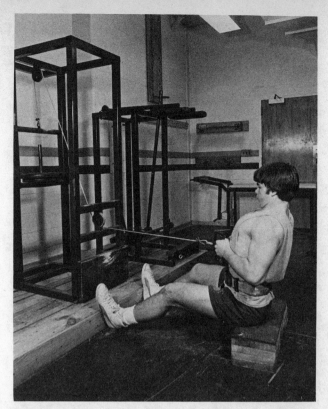

Simultaneously bend your arms to bring the handle towards you and bend the back backwards at the hip. Pull the handle towards the torso until it touches it, then slowly return the handles to the initial position. Notice that the arms are kept close to the body during the exercise.

Seated rows are great for the muscles of the upper back and they also work the biceps and forearms. At the start of the exercise (shown here), stretch as far forward as possible while keeping the knees bent.

backward or forward at the waist, keeping the back straight and the chest out. Inhale, perform the pull, and exhale as you return to the initial starting position.

Behind Neck Pulldown

Grip the bar in an overhand manner with hands approximately thirty inches apart. Sit down until you are in full support of the poundage being handled, with arms extended overhead. Inhale deeply and pull the bar down behind your head to the middle of the traps. Return slowly to the starting position and exhale. Again, think about the back, not the biceps.

Seated Pulldown to Chest

Grip the handles of a lat machine, using a wide bar with the hands about 36 inches apart. Sit until you are in the extended arm position while in complete support of the weight stack. Keep the head up, leaning back slightly and watching the pulley path at all times. Inhale deeply, pulling the bar down to

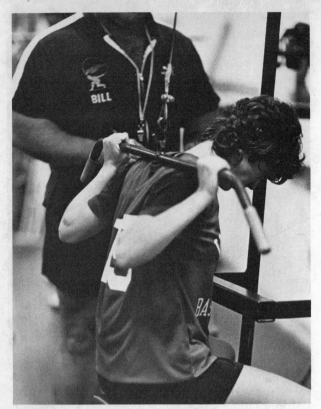

The behind-the-neck pulldown (also known as lat pulls) is a good exercise for those too weak to do a full set of chin-ups. Pulldowns help the back muscles. Notice the trainee's overhand grip and the fact that she brings the bar down to her shoulder blades.

Seated chest pulldowns also develop the latissimus dorsi muscles. Shown here is the starting position of the exercise. Notice that the head is tilted up throughout the exercise.

Chest pulldowns—finishing position. Use a variety of the exercises shown in this book to develop your lat muscles, to avoid boredom, and to best suit your own body type.

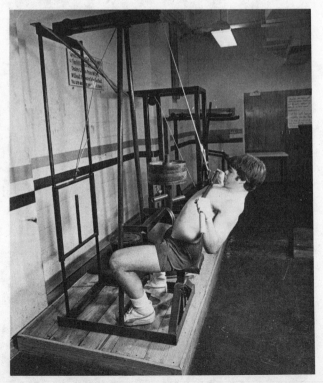

just above the nipples. Hold momentarily, then slowly ease the weight back, exhale, and repeat.

Cable Curls

Stand between a cable crossover machine, double wall-high pulleys, or a seated row machine (button position) and grip the handles. Lift the elbows very high, inhale, and with biceps strength, curl the weight stack in toward your head. Hold the contracted position for a moment, ease back, exhale, and repeat.

Hammer Curls

Sit on a flat bench, preferably a narrow one, with a dumbbell on each side, feet directly under the knees. Grip each weight with a "palms in" and "thumbs up" position, while

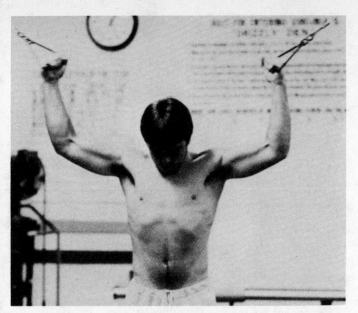

Cable curls strengthen your biceps. Shown here is the midpoint of the exercise. Note how the elbows are kept high.

Hammer curls are an excellent dumbbell curl which allows the trainee to concentrate on each arm separately or jointly. While curling the weight, don't flare the elbows back and make sure to keep the feet under the knees. Shown here is the starting position of the exercise.

Hammer curls—middle of the exercise.

Hammer curls—finish position.

keeping the chest out, the shoulders up, and the back straight. Without allowing the elbows to flare back, inhale deeply and curl the dumbbells up. Exhale, then lower slowly, and repeat.

Triceps Push

Lie on a flat bench, feet up on the end. Gripping an Olympic EZ-curl bar, use a "false grip" with palms out, thumbs under. The grip should be about 4 inches apart, thumb to thumb. Take a hand off, inhale deeply, and drive the bar up to a lockout. Exhale, lower the chin, and repeat. When at the bottom position, the bar should be close to the chin.

Triceps Pushdown

Stand erect in front of a lat pulldown machine. Grip the bar with the palms down, about 10 inches apart. Keeping the elbows tucked in close to your sides, lower the bar until your arms are fully extended. Inhale deeply at the beginning of the lift; then, as you pass the point of the greatest resistance, begin to exhale. Ease the weight down slowly, but do not relax.

The triceps push is a fine barbell exercise for the arms. Notice that during this exercise, the legs are bent, with the feet resting on the bench, and that the palms face up. Shown here is the starting position of the exercise. This exercise isolates the triceps muscles very effectively.

The triceps pushdown develops the entire tricep muscle group. Notice that the trainee uses a "false" grip, with the thumbs pointed down.

Dips

Using parallel bars or a dip stand (strapping additional weight on with a webbed belt or rope if necessary or desirable), position yourself on the bars so that the arms and shoulders are completely supporting the body weight. Breathe normally. Be sure that the feet do not touch the floor at any time. Keep the elbows out to the side while lowering downward by bending the arms. Drop until the forearms and biceps come together, pause, and press back to lockout, forcing an extension of the triceps. Do not swing back and forth.

Chins

Be sure to use a ladder or chinning bar that is at least 6 inches above your arms' extended reach. Jump up and grip the bar with the palms (either in or out, depending on results desired) about 18 inches apart. Inhale deeply and pull up until the chin is above the bar or ladder. Return to a fully extended position, exhale, and repeat.

A spotter is useful in reducing the swaying movement.

Abdominal Hangs

	Test Hang Time
Fair	40 seconds
Good	50 seconds
Excellent	60 seconds or more

Leg raises from a chinning bar or ladder are superior for strengthening the abdomen (especially the lower section), low back, hips, and

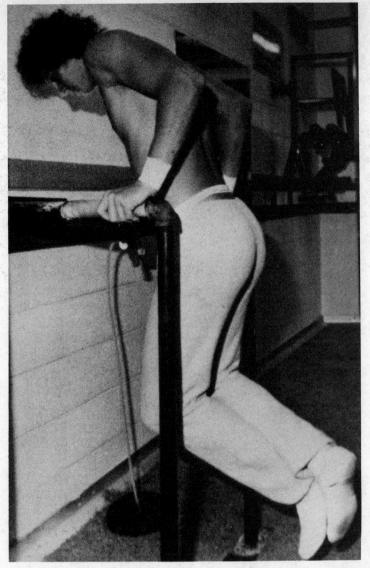

Shown here being done with an outside close grip, chin-ups can be done in a variety of ways. To fully develop the lat muscles, be sure to keep the back arched so that the lat muscle can fully contract.

Dips are a simple way to develop the triceps. Raise and lower the body by extending your arms. Be careful not to swing back and forth.

upper thigh area. Hang from the bar with a partner pushing in on your lower back to steady and support you. Then, while squeezing the bar as tightly as possible, raise the legs as high as you can and hold. Remember to keep them straight. Hold for a count of six seconds (to start with), gradually increasing the seconds. Lower very slowly in a strict fashion, then raise again. Then a set of knees-up crunches. Concentrate every second.

Dead Lift

This is a lift that is not used a great deal in strength training for basketball, although it is one of the major power-building exercises in weightlifting. We include it here because building up the thigh, hip, and buttock muscles is so important in rebounding and jumping.

On all but the heaviest sets, an overhand grip is used, because the normal reverse grip puts the body in an unnatural twisting position. Straps can also be used to secure a better grip.

Because leverage on all lifts is crucial, keep the bar close to your body at all times. Remember that the arms are longest in a straight-shoulder hanging position. Keep the line of vertebrae straight at all times.

Other than these points, the technique is exactly the same as in power cleans and high

Hanging out at the gym can be great for you. Abdominal hangs are a tremendous way to strengthen the lower abdomen. Notice how the trainee's partner holds him in the correct position.

Shown in these photographs is the dead lift, "sumo" and "conventional" style. Both styles are great for building the lower back, hip, thigh, and upper back muscles. Notice that the trainee, employing the "sumo" style, uses an overhand grip.

"Sumo" dead lift—near the finishing position.

"Sumo" dead lift—finishing position.

Conventional dead lift—near the starting position. Notice the use of the reverse grip.

Conventional style dead lift—finishing position.

The following three photographs show the correct position of the back during the dead lift. Notice that at the start, the shoulders are over the bar.

Above—the midpoint of the dead lift. As in the beginning of the clean, the arms are kept extended at full length.

Dead lift—finishing position. Notice that the bar is held close to the body during the lift for maximum leverage.

pulls, except that you merely stand erect (shoulders back) with the bar to complete the lift.

The side views below illustrate the correct position of the back throughout the lift. Notice the shoulders are over the bar.

Incline Dumbbell Press

For clarity, the accompanying photographs show only one spotter, but if at all possible two should be involved. The spotters should hand the dumbbells off to the lifter at the bottom position. The lifter should inhale just before receiving the bells, then drive the weights up and back, stopping directly above the bridge of the nose.

Exhale as you pass the point of greatest resistance. Inhale, and repeat. Be sure to keep the weights close to your body and turned at a slight angle (see photos). This is a great exercise and should always be performed after regular bench presses.

Flys

This exercise works the part of the body to which the deltoid (shoulder) and pectoral (chest) muscles attach. Isolate this area by propping the feet up and, whenever possible, use a narrow bench, to allow for greater range of motion. Again, use two spotters. Inhale, take the dumbbells in a "palms-in" position and at arms' length. With elbows bent, ease the bells down with complete control (slowly), chest high. Then explode the bells up to lockout (above the eyes), exhaling just beyond the point of greatest difficulty. Lockout, inhale, and repeat.

These additional exercises should always be performed for ten repetitions regardless of

The incline dumbbell press stresses the upper pectoral and front deltoid muscles. A spotter is necessary to give the weight to the trainee at the starting position.

Incline dumbbell press—midpoint position. Notice that the weights are kept close to the body at all times.

Incline dumbbell press—finish position. Unlike the bench press, the dumbbell press allows the trainee to lower the weight below the chest for greater muscle benefit.

Flys develop the part of the body where the deltoid and pectoral muscles attach. Notice that the feet of the trainee rest on the bench.

the cycle phase. The exercises can be added or deleted and the number of sets can be varied (but never more than three) depending on individual need.

In selecting which of these extra exercises to perform and how many sets, we suggest you refer back to the results of your initial testing and evaluation session. For example, if these tests indicate a deficiency (imbalance) in the hamstring area of the legs (should be 50/50), you should add three sets of hamstring curls to your program, instead of just one or two, until the imbalance is corrected. Also, many basketball players are proportionately weak in the low back area, and adding extra work in the various rowing movements listed in the upper body chart will correct the problem.

Unless an obvious need dictates different measures, you should perform each upper body assistant movement listed for two sets of ten repetitions during the first eight weeks

of training (foundation and preparation phases) and for one set of ten reps during the final three weeks before maxing out (precompetition phase). During the in-season (maintenance phase), omit all of those upper body assistants listed above except parallel squats, hip sleds, power cleans, and concentration rows.

Regarding the lower body, the first three phases should include parallel squats, hip sleds, power cleans, and high pulls for two sets of the appropriate repetitions. During the competitive season, high pulls should be substituted for squats, thereby reducing the stress on the lower back area. However, unlike the upper body, sets on these lower-extremity exercises should be limited to two or, in some cases, three.

Points for More Advanced Athletes

Obviously, more advanced players will start workouts at a considerably higher level than merely lifting the bar with no weights. The principles remain the same, however, with a few exceptions, which are:

1. In the initial four weeks, advanced athletes should do a higher volume of work (add one set to every exercise already outlined).
2. In addition, wherever possible (in the bench press and fly (dumbbells) exercises, for example) advanced athletes should keep their feet up on the end of the bench (or on a chair) in order to better isolate the muscles being worked. When bench pressing in this manner, be sure to lower each repetition to different points on your chest to better develop the entire pectoral region. Utilizing closer and wider hand spacing on alternate workouts (e.g., 2 inches closer or wider hand grip than normal) will also open additional adaptive response from these muscles.
3. The final point for advanced trainees in selecting supplemental exercises is to be sure that each muscle group involved in the major lifts receives individual work.

For example, the bench press involves lats (back), pectorals (inner and outer chest), triceps, and deltoids (shoulders). Each area must be thoroughly conditioned.

Advanced athletes especially, at the conclusion of every workout, must know beyond any doubt that they are precisely on schedule for achieving all goals, both long-range as well as short-term. This is very, very important.

SELECTING WORKOUT POUNDAGES

The question we are most often asked about specific lifts and poundages is, "How can I determine where to start?"

We suggested specific lifts in Chapter 6. Selecting appropriate poundages is the final area of preparation before beginning your first 11-week cycle.

The importance of this one point is of such magnitude that even if an athlete adhered strictly to everything else we have covered, but erred in just this one area, frustration and failure would almost surely be the result. For this reason, we will now cover, as carefully and clearly as possible, selecting workout poundages.

The first four weeks of your cycle constitute the foundation phase in which the physical base for the season is established.

After warm-up and stretching, beginning with an Olympic bar (45 pounds) and no weights, perform consecutive sets of 10 strict repetitions, adding weight with each set, until you reach the top poundage which you can comfortably handle for all 10 repetitions. This is to be the top set for that day. The weight increment between sets for beginners should be 2½ pounds; for women and men through high school age the increase should be five pounds. For college-aged men, the poundage jump between sets is ten pounds. This holds true for all upper body lifts (the bench press, for example). On lower-extremity exercises, which involve the larger and stronger thigh, hip, buttock, and back muscles (squats, for example), the increment

should be 10 pounds for women and 20 pounds for men.

It cannot be too strongly emphasized that you are never to increase any poundage being lifted until all 10 repetitions have been satisfactorily completed in strict form.

Again, remember that strength increases come *from* training and not *when* training. So work hard, but also be patient with yourself. Maximum effort is the key. Only add weight on upper body exercises at the rate of 5 pounds at a time, 10 pounds on lower-body movement. This is after the initial workout poundages have been arrived at (as outlined). If you train properly, the ability to handle these increases will occur weekly.

Where you start, in terms of how strong you are at the outset, is not of major importance. It is where you are going, and being sure you get there, that is important.

On major upper body lifts such as the bench press, power clean, and high pull, players can realistically expect to add between 20 and 25 pounds per cycle. Poundages for lower body movements, such as squats and leg presses, can be expected to increase by 35 to 40 pounds per cycle.

A rule of thumb for estimating the poundages that can be lifted during a workout is that for each repetition (in a multiple repetition set), 10 pounds can be applied to any other set with higher or lower poundage. This means that if you perform 10 repetitions with 100 pounds, you will almost always be able to handle a single lift with 200 pounds. Or, if you lift 200 pounds for a triple (three times), you could perform a single with 230 pounds.

When any given day's workout is completed, you must know and believe with total conviction that you are right on schedule for achieving all goals. You must realize beyond a shadow of a doubt that whatever your top poundage of the day, your achievement put you directly on target. Furthermore you know that you have worked your hardest to reach your potential as a basketball player.

And finally, at the end of each workout, you should go over, in your own mind, exactly what you will be demanding of your body during the next workout, including every lift, set, repetition, poundage, and exercise. *If you want to enjoy continuous progress, you must not skip any of these stages.* When working out in the manner described above, you can be sure that each subsequent cycle will set you on course for a higher level of fitness for basketball.

SELECTING AND CHARTING YOUR CYCLE GOALS

For recording daily progress, two logs are necessary. The first is the daily workout log discussed in Chapter 3. The second is the guide for the daily workout session, showing the goals for each day, week, cycle phase, and max-out (ultimate goal). In the Appendix you'll find blank logs, (so that you may fill in your own poundages), as well as Ralph Sampson's actual charts, which detail his strength training program. Please don't try to imitate his results unless you're well-prepared.

As we mentioned earlier, use a more limited program during the in-season in terms of time in the weightroom, in order to conserve strength for playing basketball, while maintaining all or as much as possible of the strength gained earlier. This involves two workouts per week—one heavy session and one very high-intensity circuit workout. Conditioning during the competitive season is, of course, handled by the basketball coaches. The workout logs at the end of Chapter 3 show the specific exercises, poundages, and repetitions we suggest performing during this time. However, as a rule of thumb, for the circuit sessions in which the primary exercises are performed for 30-second intervals, athletes should use poundages that are roughly 50 percent of their maximum single repetition for all sets. The heavy day should conform to previously mentioned guidelines. Whatever you do, never omit in-season training.

More than muscles alone win basketball games. Terry Holland, head coach of the Virginia basketball team, and Coach Dunn time members of the team to improve their power, speed, and conditioning.

8
CONDITIONING FACTORS

You're reading this book because you want to become a better basketball player; we want to help you achieve that goal. We've talked about how to enhance your strength, and you can see why that aspect of training is so essential. However, strength training must be combined with good conditioning if you really hope to excel on the basketball court. Building the "body beautiful" is very important, but it's only one aspect of training.

Conditioning—endurance, coordination, agility, etc.—is the other aspect of the multifaceted training program we are outlining here. This program, when fully implemented, is indeed a winner. Ralph can tell you that.

THE FUNDAMENTALS OF CONDITIONING

Each of these is essential. A player with good coordination but poor endurance is going to get beaten out on the court. Your training program must include each of these.

Power

This is vital in basketball. Therefore, not only strengthening of muscles, but increasing the ability of the muscles to contract at a faster and more explosive rate, is mandatory.

Muscular Endurance

This must be increased because basketball players need to sustain powerful muscle contractions for extended periods of effort.

Strength Training

This is important in creating a strong base from which power and muscular endurance may be built.

Cardiovascular Endurance

Developing and maintaining a high level of cardiovascular endurance (physical working power) will also be a great benefit. Cardiovascular (cardiorespiratory) endurance is the result of conditioning the entire body, and improving the flow of oxygen to the muscles. It differs from muscular endurance in that it is not localized or restricted to a specific muscle or group of muscles. Doing chin-ups, for example, will improve muscular endurance but not cardiovascular endurance.

Improved cardiovascular endurance will:

- provide the fundamental base for all other conditioning;
- enable an athlete to perform work with less energy expenditure;
- help delay fatigue.

Aerobic Training

This provides the base that must be built first. It is the form of cardiovascular work that basketball players should do during the foundation phase of their cycles. This type of training includes continuous long-distance and medium-distance running (3–5 miles per workout), raising the pulse rate above 125 beats per minute, and sustaining this rate for at least 20–30 minutes.

Anaerobic Training

This is the most vital part of conditioning for basketball, since it is a sport requiring relatively short but very explosive bursts of energy. While some aerobic training is necessary (for establishing a base), we feel strongly that the major means of providing muscle energy for basketball is nonoxidative or anaerobic training. Why? Because it is speed, explosive anaerobic speed, that is necessary for basketball. This is why the agility drills and interval 220-yard sprint drills that we will soon outline are so important. These types of interval power training are necessary from the standpoint of specificity, to allow adequate recovery between training exercises so that all movements can be performed at or near the actual competitive speed at which basketball is played.

Hand-Eye Coordination

This is another very fundamental aspect of

basketball that must be improved in training. In previous chapters we indirectly mentioned several pertinent points about hand-eye coordination one of which was the need for "right thinking." To perform any physical function well requires an athlete's body parts to function in a cohesive manner, with balance, control, and the highest level of concentration possible. The basketball itself must become an extension of your torso, arms, hands, fingertips, even nerve endings. When shooting, it is as if you were actually putting your own hand into the cylinder. This is one of the reasons that the mental factor is so important. We also mentioned the need for balance and control in Chapter 6. In addition to the agility drills which will be outlined shortly, the primary drill which we use at the University of Virginia for improving hand-eye coordination is one in which four players, three of whom have a basketball, stand in a half-circle, with one other teammate about ten feet out in front of them without a ball. On command, one of the four alternately passes or bounces the ball to the player in the center, who returns it, although not necessarily to the original player. This drill continues for one full minute, at which time the players alternate positions.

Running Speed

Speed is the result of applying force to mass. That is why we must work to strengthen the muscles used in running, so that they will be capable of applying greater force, bringing about an increase in movement.

Three factors combine to create foot speed:

1. strength-coordinated muscle contraction and relaxation
2. stride length
3. stride frequency

These points demonstrate another need for the testing and evaluation sessions mentioned at the outset of Chapter 1. Coordination between the contracting and the relaxing muscle groups will help increase speed of movement. Keeping muscles in proper balance as strength increases is the primary prerequisite for developing muscular ability to exert maximum force at extreme ranges of motion, and doing so at the fastest possible rate of speed.

The key point is that all muscles must be strengthened and kept in balance at the same time. In other words, stride length can't be improved at the expense of stride frequency. Another very important point is that arm strength is often the limiting factor in increasing speed, rather than leg power. For example, if the arm speed is not improved via strength training, the athlete's speed slows due to nonsyncrony and neuro-muscular inhibition. It has also been found that the hamstring/quadriceps relationship should be 50/50, not 60/40 as we thought for so many years.

In accordance with the gradual peaking principles of periodization over the course of a cycle, we suggest a wide assortment of running and agility drills be used. Especially effective are running and form-related types of drills that require high knee action, crossing over while keeping straight hip alignment, touching heels to buttocks, back pedaling, and assorted jump rope drills.

Regarding running form, the following points should be considered:

Proper Mechanics	Improper Mechanics
Body erect	Leaning forward
Chest and head up	Chest and head down
Eyes forward	Eyes down
Arm swing vigorous	Arm swing excessive
Arm swing parallel	Arm swing across chest
No back kick	Back kick
Rock up on toes	Flat-footed run
High knee action	Little knee action

Keep in mind that just as you do not have to lift maximum poundages at all times to make progress, neither do you need to run all out, at all times, to develop the capacity to do so. Putting reasonable emphasis on running techniques is often a great benefit in learning how to run properly at great speeds.

Such little "tricks" as always running off-season outside drills with the wind at your back and appropriate downhill sprint work are two very effective training practices.

After practice or workouts it is often helpful to massage the feet vigorously as tightness and tenseness can build up in these lower extremities. Here again, PNF stretching is important.

During the first four weeks (foundation phase) of a cycle, basketball players should run cross-country for a distance of:

1. Week 1: 3 miles
2. Week 2: 4 miles
3. Week 3: 5 miles
4. Week 4: 5 miles

These runs should be at a low speed, and run early in the morning three days per week, preferably on nonlifting days, although this is not mandatory. This will begin to establish a new fitness base (remember that the high-repetition lifting is also preparing a base). This is the bottom of the pyramid. Do not skip these runs even if you must crawl out to the track or cross-country course. If a base is not established, failure will be the result.

At the beginning of the preparation phase (second four weeks), the long-distance running begun in the first phase should be cut down to one run of a maximum distance the athlete can run in 12 minutes. This means picking up the intensity (speed) even though decreasing the distance.

Agilities and interval sprints should be worked into the program at this time as well. Agilities are performed after warm-up and stretching, but always before running. Interval sprints are very important—specifically, running 220-yard sprints beginning with three the first week. These are to be run and always timed, on Tuesday and Saturday, between strength training workouts. The 12 minute run is to be worked in between the sprints (on Thursday) which are increased by two each week (the progression is 5-7-9-11-13-15) until fifteen are run during the seventh week, the last week of the pre-competition phase.

Regarding the interval 220-yard sprints, the following points are important. The primary emphasis on these sprints is not on all-out, full-speed running, but rather that each sprint be achieved in 30 seconds or less for forwards and centers and 28 seconds or less for guards. All athletes should have a 75 second rest interval between each sprint. Any player who fails to make his required time should have a penalty added on a one-for-one basis. Be sure to start from a 5 yard walk/jog to avoid pulled muscles; do not sit down between sprints. Stand and walk around.

The primary benefit of these forced interval runs is that more work (and higher quality work) can be performed than in other types of running. Less lactic acid is built up than when running continuously, enabling players to train at much greater intensity and for extended periods of time.

We suggest running coliseum or stadium steps for 10 minutes at the conclusion of each running workout (in phases two and three). Run these under control but at full speed (hitting every step) going up, easing down, full speed again, etc.

Stretching and abdominal hangs should be performed after every workout, in or out of the weightroom.

As shown in the illustrations below, always use a partner when doing abdominal hangs. The partner you stretch out with is best because he or she is attuned to your body and needs, can give commands, and can support the lower back, as well as help to raise the legs, if and when necessary. Start with front, right, left, front raises, all for 6 seconds, and work up slowly to 12 seconds each way over a period of several weeks. Increase as often as possible. Also, start with one set and work up to three full sets, moving immediately on to the cool-down at the completion of these exercises.

Agility and Quickness

These drills round out our conditioning program. Ideally, agilities should involve the skill movements necessary to play basketball. We suggest 10 minutes of jumping rope after stretching, using various speeds and footwork, then moving on to agilities, and then to the day's running work. Also, during the short rest intervals, try mentally to bring your own pulse rate under control as quickly as possible, rather than letting your minds wander.

All agilities should be timed. We recommend selecting ten of those suggested, alternating one jumping agility with one sliding/balance agility. Time these for 30 seconds, with 10 second rests between each one. It makes no difference with which agility you begin, providing all ten are performed. The accompanying illustrations show the ones we most often use.

Before making some final comments on conditioning, let's look briefly at just how the strength training and conditioning workouts blend together over the course of the 11 weeks of a cycle.

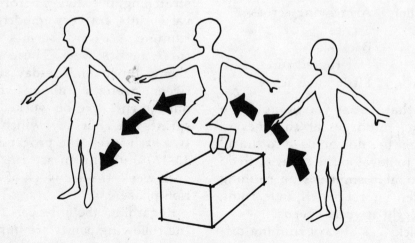

Jump over pad (Jumping drill)

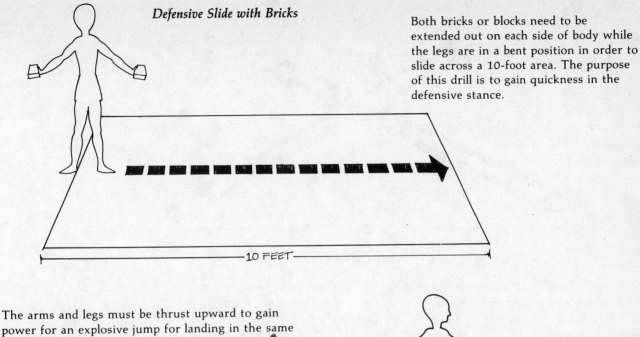

Defensive Slide with Bricks

Both bricks or blocks need to be extended out on each side of body while the legs are in a bent position in order to slide across a 10-foot area. The purpose of this drill is to gain quickness in the defensive stance.

10 FEET

The arms and legs must be thrust upward to gain power for an explosive jump for landing in the same position as that at the beginning of the exercise. The purpose of the drill is to acquire quickness in the repetitive jumping used throughout a basketball game.

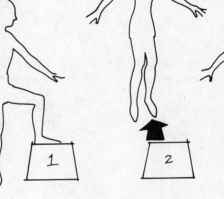

Bench Blast

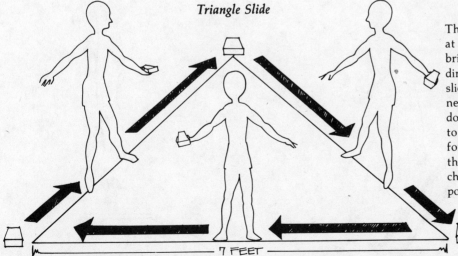

Triangle Slide

Three bricks or blocks are used, one at each corner of the triangle. A brick is placed in the hand of the direction. The athlete is defensively sliding until he or she reaches the next brick; the first brick is placed down, and the second brick is used to continue on in the sliding position for the next brick. The purpose of this drill is to gain quickness for changing directions in the defensive position.

7 FEET

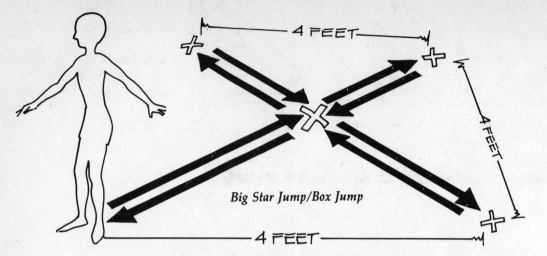

Big Star Jump/Box Jump

Start at one end of the star and jump to the middle star, then to the next point of the star and, again, back to the middle. Each time a jump is made *away* from the middle, a jump needs to be made *back* to the middle in order to get a triangle effect. This drill is used for quickness in jumping for different positions that the body needs to use during the course of a game.

The brick is placed in front of the body in order to slide in a forward motion toward the opposite brick. The brick is placed down to pick up the other brick for the next slide toward the opposite direction. The purpose of this drill is to gain a quicker and longer stride for running and sliding.

The beep board is used for explosive and consecutive leaps toward the basket. The body needs to extend as much to the basket as possible. This drill is used for jumping in order to rebound the basketball.

Up-and-Back Slide

Jump Touch with Beep Board

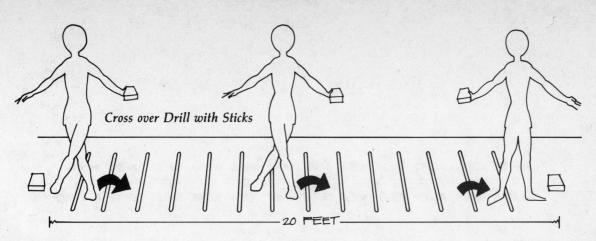

Cross over Drill with Sticks

20 FEET

The legs perform cross over motion while one brick (held in the hand of the direction the body is moving) is placed down in order to pick up another and continue back in the opposite direction. This exercise is for quickness of feet.

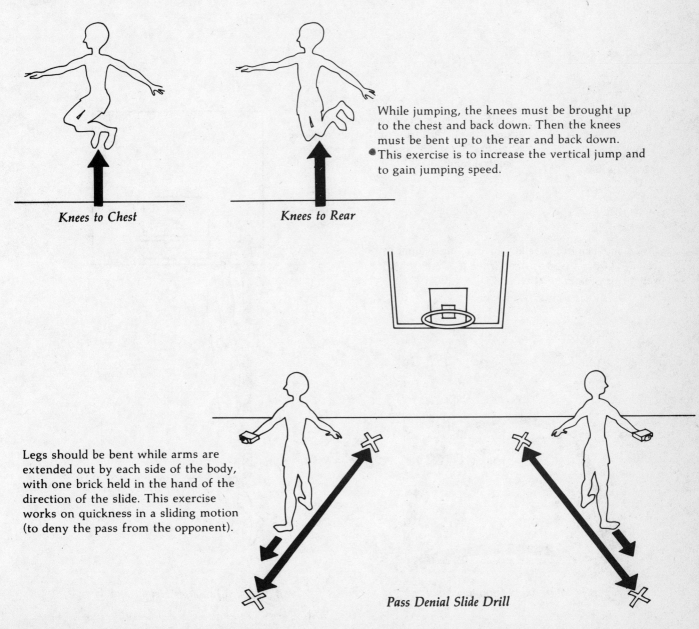

Knees to Chest

Knees to Rear

While jumping, the knees must be brought up to the chest and back down. Then the knees must be bent up to the rear and back down. This exercise is to increase the vertical jump and to gain jumping speed.

Legs should be bent while arms are extended out by each side of the body, with one brick held in the hand of the direction of the slide. This exercise works on quickness in a sliding motion (to deny the pass from the opponent).

Pass Denial Slide Drill

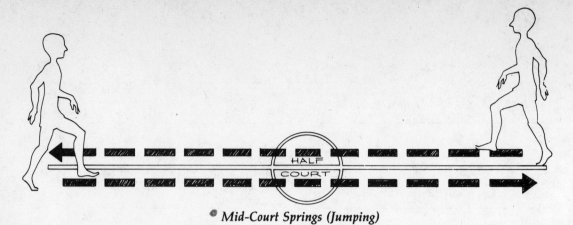

Mid-Court Springs (Jumping)

Start at one end of the half-court line and sprint to the other side as fast as possible. This should be continued until time has elapsed. The sprints promote quickness for running the full length of the court at a game's pace.

Consecutive jumping is needed in order to touch the backboard or other such desired heights. This agility is used to increase vertical jump.

Quick movement is needed for jumping around in the square. Drill is used to strengthen legs and to gain repetitive jumping ability.

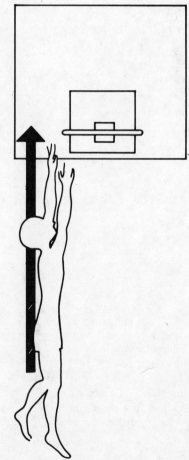

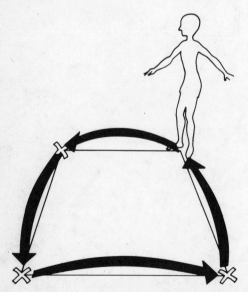

Big Square Jump (Jumping Drill)

Blackboard Jump for Height and Time

Two people are facing each other approximately 4 feet apart as they rapidly use a chest pass to throw a medicine ball back and forth. This drill is used for eye coordination, strength, and quickness.

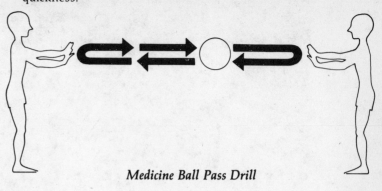

Back-to-Back Medicine ball (Balance/Quickness)

Two people must be faced back-to-back while they quickly pass a medicine ball around each other's waists. This drill is used for balance and quickness.

Medicine Ball Pass Drill

Use both feet to explode over each of the bags by using the momentum of arms and legs. This drill is important for quick jumping and also helps to strengthen legs.

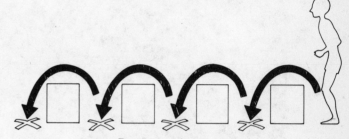

Bag Jumps for Height

Before making some final comments on conditioning, let's look briefly at just how the strength training and conditioning workouts blend together over the course of the 11 weeks of a cycle.

CYCLE PHASE	STRENGTH TRAINING	CONDITIONING WORK	GOAL
1—Foundation 4—Weeks	High volume work High Repetition Lifting (General work)	High volume work Long distance running (General Work)	Fitness Base
2—Preparation 4—weeks	Medium volume work Higher intensity—mid-range reps in lifting (Specific works)	Medium volume work Higher intensity 12 min. run Agilities—220 yd. Sprints begin (Specific work)	Basic Strength
3—Pre-Competition 3—weeks	Low volume work Asst. exercises reduced Very high intensity Low reps but heavy weights—ending in Max-out (Very specific work)	Low volume work Very high intensity High Event participation (basketball) Agilities, springs All-out efforts. (Very specific work)	Strength Power
4—In-Season Maintenance	Low volume (2 workouts per wk) Lower intensity— 70-80% of maximum load	On court Conditioning by Coaches	Win Basketball Games
	(Totally Sport Spec. Work)	(Totally Sport Spec. Work)	

He doesn't do it with mirrors: Pro football star Pat Chester stretches out for the vertical jump test.

9

INCREASING THE VERTICAL JUMP AND PASSING PROFICIENCY

Two of the questions most frequently asked of a strength coach affiliated with a successful basketball program are, "How may vertical jumping ability be increased?" and "How may passing proficiency be improved?" Since both of these important skills can be dramatically improved, let's look at just how these changes are accomplished.

MEASURING VERTICAL JUMP

As the pictures indicate, we use a large rectangular plywood board of 7 feet in length by 2 feet in width, sanded smooth and painted white. We mark ours for height, beginning at 6 feet and then, ½ inch at a time, up to a maximum of 13 feet (to allow for "moon" jumps like Ralph Sampson's).

This board should be in a very brightly lit and uncluttered area, mounted out from the wall about eight inches, enabling players to jump straight up and not against the wall. We recommend grading vertical leaps on the following scale:

To measure the vertical leap (after warm-up, jump rope, and stretching) stand flat-footed next to or below the board and obtain your maximum reach. Then, with the inside foot nearest the wall and the other foot slightly back, propel yourself out of a crouch, reaching to the highest possible point on the board. We suggest recording three efforts, with the "best leap" being the average of the three. The reason for recording the average rather than the highest jump is that basketball players must develop the ability not only to jump higher and higher, but also to attain limited heights in rapid succession.

Most athletes, with proper work and conscientious effort, may expect dramatic increases of 3–4 inches per year, particularly if they are training while still growing. We recommend testing vertical jumps at the beginning and end of each cycle phase—in other words, at 4-week, 4-week, and 3-week intervals, coinciding with the 11 weeks of foundation, preparation, and pre-competition phases.

IMPROVING VERTICAL LEAPING ABILITY

In general, an increase in the vertical jump can be achieved through a combination of:

1. Strength training
2. Comprehensive conditioning
3. Depth jumping (bounding/plyometrics)

Strength training, discussed in the last chapter, adds size to muscles, tendons, and ligaments, and is essential in the development of "raw" strength. It is particularly important for the development of the "rotary hip" movement, the act of consistantly bringing the legs and hips under the body in a maximum power position—something many athletes fail to do. This movement will propel the body up rather than out (as when the back is used improperly). When the lower back becomes the prime mover, rather than the legs, thighs, and hips, full power and maximum extension are not achieved, thereby limiting the height of the leap.

Mastering this rotary hip movement is not easy, but it is vital for the improvement of jumping ability. Not only basketball, but many other sports, among them football, require mastery of this technique. For this reason, we suggest full squats along with power cleans and high pulls, always starting with light poundages (the Olympic bar alone is best). Refer to Chapter 6 for the correct techniques on these exercises.

Conditioning factors have been discussed at length in Chapter 8. Such factors as leg lift, leg kick, stride length, and power arm movements are all vital aspects of great jumping increases. Remember that all strength training and conditioning training is inseparably linked to increases in overall performance, not just jumping ability.

In addition to the points just mentioned, we suggest that various depth-jumping drills be worked into your program, after weightroom workouts, twice per week during the off-season (first two cycle phases only), and for a total of 12 to 15 minutes each session.

Maybe Ralph Sampson can reach 9'3" without jumping, but you should build your skills so that you can improve your vertical jump.

Depth-jumping is a relatively new concept in America, but it has been used to great advantage in the Soviet Union and in East Germany for a wide variety of sports. This type of training increases the explosiveness of the leg muscles. The Russian strength expert Y. Uzlow puts it this way:

"Pure strength (for the legs) is developed mainly by weight training exercises; dynamic strength by . . . depth-jumping and repetition [of] hops and bounds."

Developing a player's maximum vertical jump is of tremendous importance to basketball players. Here the members of the UVA women's basketball team demonstrate several drills which improve vertical jumping and build explosiveness and strength.

ADDING BODY WEIGHT

Most athletic supply stores carry light attachable weights (for ankles and waist). These are very helpful in developing jumping ability. Weights, however, should only be added after the skills being discussed are properly mastered. We recommend 2½-pound weights for the ankles and a 5 pound (beginning) vest for the waist.

When you first begin to use weights, you should start in the following manner:

1. Perform five sets of 30-second running-in-place drills (with ankle weights attached), with a 30-second rest interval between sets.

Emphasize high knee lift, relaxation, and good running form.

Increase the intensity of each set until the fourth and fifth sets are performed at full speed.

2. The second drill is performed immediately after the first one, by adding the 5 pound weighted vest and performing a series (3 sets of 10 repetitions) of depth jumps.

Jump down from a bench (12 inches to begin with) facing the bench, and immediately explode back up on the bench. These movements should be performed with maximum intensity and effort, with a 60-second interval between each set.

• Benches of 12, 16, and 20 inches should be used (later increasing to 24-, 26-, and 30-inch boxes).

• The scientific principle of depth-jumping is that a concentric (i.e., shortening) contraction is much stronger if it immediately follows an eccentric (i.e., lengthening) contraction of the same muscle. An eccentric contraction occurs when a muscle is loaded sufficiently to lengthen it, even though at the same time it is trying to shorten. In the language of basketball, this means that when a player is performing a vertical jump, the initial movement is downward to pre-stretch the quadriceps. This downward or pre-stretching movement stores mechanical energy in the contracted muscle, which is released during the subsequent shortening contraction (the jump). This contraction will propel the player higher than if there were no prior downward (pre-stretching) movement. (See illustrations on pages 76–79.)

Depth-jumping is governed by principles similar to those of PNF Stretching. Remember, when a muscle is suddenly stretched, it almost instantaneously contracts to resist that stretch. A signal is being picked up by the alpha motor nerve in the spinal column, which in turn sends the command to contract. This process of signal transmission between the muscle spindle and alpha motor nerve can be accelerated through training (i.e., depth-jumping or bounding), so that the muscle reacts more quickly when it is put into the stretch position.

1. Lengthening contraction of leg muscles

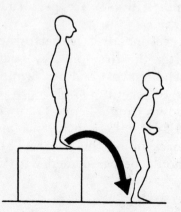

2. Shortening contraction of leg muscles

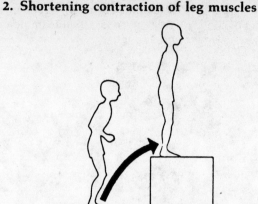

The faster the transition from 1 to 2, the greater the tension in the concentric contraction and, therefore, the greater the momentary load on the jumping muscles.

The basic equipment for depth-jumping exercises is as follows:

- several wooden boxes, varying in height from 18 inches to 30 inches (you can make these yourself);
- one or two soft gym mats (to make the landing softer and avoid traumatizing the knee joints).

In performing the depth-jump exercises, consider the following very important points:

1. Depth-jumps must not be performed during the competition season.
2. Discontinue depth-jumping exercises at the end of the off-season preparation workout cycle.
3. Depth-jumps are potentially dangerous, the height of the jump-off boxes must be adjusted to the strength level of each athlete.
4. (a) During the first four weeks of the first cycle (foundation period), perform depth jumps from lower boxes (18–24 inches). During this period, strengthen your legs with free weights (squats) and various machines mentioned in the last chapter.
   (b) During the second four weeks of the cycle (preparation), perform depth-jumps only twice a week, working up to the highest possible boxes.
5. Always jump onto a soft mat.

6. Avoid arm movements. Any swinging movement of the arms leads to a transfer of momentum from the legs into the torso and is similar to "cheating" in the weight exercises. Try to keep your hands on your hips as much as possible.

7. Do not allow your legs to "give" before rebounding. This is difficult to learn, but it is very important for achieving the maximum conditioning effect on the alpha motor nerve. The rebound (or "explosive reflex") must be immediate from legs that are in a flexed position.

8. Stop depth-jumping immediately if pain occurs in the knee joints. Never depth-jump with sore knee joints.

9. Perform 15–20 jumping combinations (as illustrated) once or twice a week, depending on cycle period and individual needs.

10. In doing forward-jumps, leap off the lower box on the mat and onto the higher box.

11. In doing reverse (about-face) jumps, leap off the higher box onto the mat and onto the lower box.

12. Use your imagination in devising depth-jump variations.

Basic Depth-Jump Exercises

Forward Jump Off-and-On Boxes

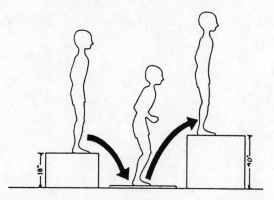

Reverse Jump Off-and On Boxes

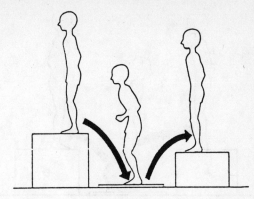

Depth-Jump Variations: The Twisted Jump

Because of the rotational aspects of many jumping movements in basketball, we also suggest adding various twisting depth-jumps to your program.

Basically, you should perform a half-twist as you leave the box or rebound off the ground:

- Half-twist jump onto Box B after jumping off Box A.

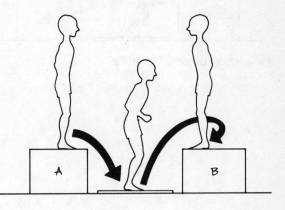

- Half-twist jump off Box A with rebound up onto Box B.

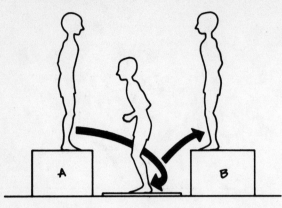

- Jump straight back off Box A; half-twist upon rebounding and land on Box B (facing opposite direction from jump-off).

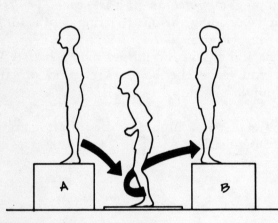

Height of Boxes: Variable

Depth-Jump Variations: One-Legged Bounding

- Jump from the lower box to the ground and onto the higher box, all on the same leg. Alter legs on next series.

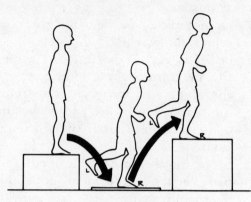

- Run up, hop on first box, jump off onto mat with same leg, and bound over second box, landing on the original jump-off leg. Reverse leg on next series.

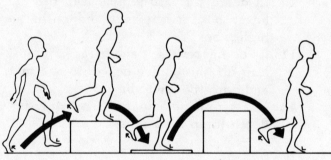

CORRECT JUMPING TECHNIQUE

Many basketball players have poor running and jumping techniques, and some of these bad habits are so ingrained that they are hard to change. So start at the beginning with light weights and technique instruction.

As far as improving running technique is concerned, refer to Chapter 7 on conditioning. It also pays to consult with a track coach.

As far as jumping is concerned, consider the points of technique emphasized in the section on the squat. The points that govern proper squatting also apply to correct jumping. Remember, above all, that a good jump results as much from hip-action as from leg and arm thrust:

WRONG TECHNIQUE

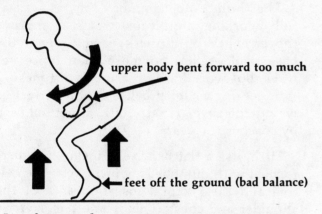

Leg thrust and arm-swing generate momentum, but leverage under gravity (c) is very poor.

CORRECT TECHNIQUE

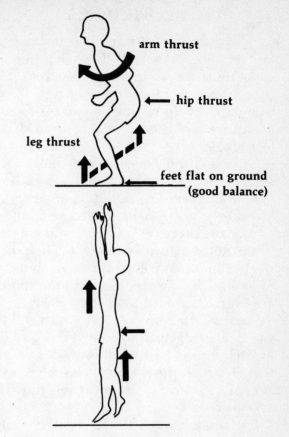

1. The hips push forward horizontally as the legs and arms thrust upward.
2. The upward momentum is increased because of better leverage under the center of gravity.

IMPROVING PASSING PROFICIENCY

Good passing skills are vital in basketball. In fact, many basketball coaches feel that shooting is actually a pass to the basket.

At any rate, a high percentage of good shots are set up by one or more passes, and passes are essential for setting up an effective fast break.

Crispness and explosive movement are important in making good passes because the harder the pass (assuming its accuracy), the less likely it is to be intercepted and the sooner the pressure is placed on the defense.

It is not the purpose of this book to discuss the techniques involved in passing, but rather to look at the muscles used and the appropriate exercise needed to develop them.

First, select from exercises which will allow the strength gained to transfer as quickly as possible to the basketball court. As we mentioned earlier, the ball must become an extension of your arm in order for this transfer to take place.

By working out with free (loose) weights your body learns to stabilize the resistance, helping to enhance good body balance.

Muscles must be placed in a state of overload to spur growth. One problem with free weights is that at certain points (six or seven inches off the chest while bench pressing, for example) the leverage is poorest, thus the overload is great. This often changes dramatically because of changing position, so as leverage position improves be very sure to continue to drive through each exercise to lockout in the most explosive manner possible, as this will keep the overload greatest, facilitating muscle growth.

Second, when working out, be sure to grip the bar, machine, or dumbbell very tightly, as this practice will not only develop grip strength, but will enhance strength gains in whatever specific muscle group is being worked at the moment.

Third, the muscles of the trunk, particularly of the lower abdominal region, including the obliques and the lower back (spinal erectors), are extremely important in passing. The abdominals should be worked every day. We suggest you do this by using the abdominal hangs discussed at the end of Chapter 6. Again, be sure to squeeze the bar or ladder.

The lower back is worked effectively using the squatting and pulling movements already described. Never work this area more than twice per week, however, and only work heavily one day per week. The second workout should not be more than an eighty percent effort on the top sets.

Fourth, be sure to include some medicine-ball drills when working on passing, being very careful to use good form and high intensity.

The thumbs-up hammer curls, as well as fully working the biceps, will also improve the strength of muscles used to pass the basketball. Again, no more than twice per week, but work hard on arms both times.

Squeezing a rubber ball is another effective way to improve grip strength, a method used by coaches for years.

Fifth, use a flat bench for incline flys performed with dumbbells, which work the deltoid and the pectoral insertion area of the shoulder and chest. This is another exercise that is extremely important. (Refer to Chapter 6 for technique explanation.)

Sixth, the best exercise is the lying triceps push (not an extension). This exercise isolates the muscles of the chest, shoulders, back, and arms as well as the wrists, and works them as a unit in almost exactly the same movement (and hand spacing) that is used to make an effective pass.

Speed and quickness drills covered in the last chapter will round out the necessary movements to make an effective transfer of muscle strength to passing proficiency.

Who is this skinny wimp? A very young Ralph Sampson tries (incorrectly) to do a power clean with a mere 155 pounds on the bar.

10
RALPH SAMPSON

There can be nothing in sports more exciting for a coach than to have the opportunity to work with a truly great athlete.

Ralph Sampson is such an athlete. Born to dominate, this special man presented a variety of special challenges to his coaches.

The pictures on pages 82 and 85 say it all. The first is a "before" snapshot of Ralph Sampson two weeks after he arrived at the University of Virginia, incorrectly attempting a power clean with 155 pounds. Notice the thin arms and chest. At 7'4" in height he weighed only a frail 193.

The second picture of the two-time NCAA Player-of-the-Year was taken after three years of work on the very program that we are outlining for you. It shows Ralph during a max-out, at a very muscular bodyweight of 230 pounds, curling in strict thumbs-up fashion 90 pound dumbbells for 10 repetitions each. This is big-time poundage for a world-class lifter, let alone a college basketball player with excessive limb length! Notice the

enormous concentration and intensity in his facial expression.

Let's go back in time and see how this incredible transformation took place.

It began in a small mountain town named Harrisonburg, nestled in the lovely Shenandoah Valley of Virginia. A boy 7'4" tall—thin, even gangly—but with mind-boggling basketball skills, was thrust into the world sports spotlight. Constantly facing all manner of trapping, sliding zone defenses, always double- and triple-teamed, Ralph Sampson nevertheless became more and more dominating. The few who tried to play head up man-to-man, he ate alive. Against one former All-American he scored 40 points and had 20 rebounds, along with numerous blocked shots.

That was the point at which people began to say that one day he would be the greatest basketball player who ever lived. He was constantly surrounded by media and fans alike, making it difficult for him to study,

Un-be-liev-able!! A Sampson in build as well as name after three years of using Coach Dunn's training program, Ralph curls a staggering 90 pounds *in each arm*, ten times!

date, and participate in normal school activities, much less be alone to think, rest, and rejuvenate. Even just sitting down to a meal, Sampson always had to wonder if he would be interrupted six, eight, or more times by autograph seekers.

Even with all his talent, he was a young man who needed time to find himself, time to grow into manhood. With a few variations, this goes on everywhere a great player trains and competes.

Greatly skilled athletes moving from high school into college often rely almost exclusively on skills. This was the case initially with Ralph Sampson. He trained, he lifted, he ran, but with nothing like an all-out commitment at first. Then, ever so gradually, Ralph began to realize that he could not be all things to all people, that he had an ultimate responsi-

bility to himself. As he did so, a change began to take place. Instead of relying on his enormous skills, he began to work very hard to overcome his weaknesses and build on his strengths—to reach out, to strive for all that Ralph Sampson's potential would allow. When he did, the results were staggering. Today , he is the Rookie-of-the-Year center for the Houston Rockets, and well on his way to becoming a living legend.

As a coach, what was it like to train Ralph Sampson? What principles are there to follow in working with any of the "great ones"? Some points always to keep in mind in working with very gifted athletes are:

1. Be absolutely sure that gifted athletes understand exactly what is being asked of them and why.

2. Talk at length about how they plan to

deal with the pressure of the press and the fans. Let them know that you fully understand the unique difficulties they face and demonstrate a sincere willingness to make whatever adjustments are necessary to help meet their needs.

3. Be encouraging, but totally frank. Let them understand that you, too, have pressures, and enormous responsibilities. For example, as Ralph's strength coach, I received at least fifteen to twenty phone calls and as many letters each week with questions about the type of program he was on. Seek to reach a common ground of communication. Go slowly.

4. Before-and-after pictures and body girth measurements are very helpful. Praise is of the utmost importance, but make them earn it. Do not flatter them with unearned rewards. Great athletes do not like to fail at anything. You must see to it that they do not fail in the weightroom.

5. Design and develop programs that will guarantee them a measure of success early.

6. Remember that athletes, even great ones, mature both physically and mentally at different times.

7. Except under very unusual circumstances, never let anyone or anything interrupt their strength training workouts. They deserve your undivided attention during this time. They must be taught the meaning of concentration and intensity. Strength training is not an added feature; it is vitally important and should be treated as such.

8. One of the most important principles to communicate to any great athlete is that of always seeking to excel, regardless of the skill level of the opposition. Once an athlete truly gets a fix on what makes himself or herself tick, he or she must not allow any outside interference, from whatever source, to dictate playing tempo. Rather, he must seek in and of himself to be the tempo-setting catalyst in all contests. This quality will move teammates and, in fact, all whose lives he or she touches, even briefly, to be inspired to reach the top themselves. Wonderful leadership quality should inspire the great basketball players, rather than making them unapproachable and conceited.

9. Coaches must demand dedication from the super athletes, the total commitment to excel, not merely in some things, but in everything. This is the opposite of their continuing to "get by" on natural ability. They will not respect those who try to cater to them. If we want them to grow into adults, we must show them the way, and then demand it. Toward the end of his first year at the university, Ralph was coming to the weightroom only every third or fourth workout. Finally, he was taken aside and frankly told that he was wasting both my time and his own and that he was not to return until he was prepared to train to be all that he could be. It made him angry, but three days later he came in and began "to go for it."

10. Help them understand that no one ever "arrives." There will always be room for improvement. Do not allow complacency to set in. Everything in life is getting better or worse, every day. We must inspire the gifted athlete to always strive to be the best—especially when there is no path to follow.

11. Every basketball player has an ideal body weight, a specific figure that will enable him to bring all physical components together in an ideal combination for success. Help him find it.

Ralph Sampson is a beautiful person—intensely loyal to family and friends. The "Big Guy" took a special interest in my oldest son and was never too busy to kid or spend a little time with him. The weightroom was a place of refuge for him; a place to get away from the endless stream of insensitive people who crossed his path.

The moral of this story is that systematic, intelligent hard work always pays off. The irony is that the "Big Guy" has only scratched the surface of his true potential. There aren't any footsteps where Ralph Sampson is heading.

APPENDIX:
CHARTS AND LOGS

VIRGINIA BASKETBALL

**Sheet #1
Interval
Sprints
and
Weights**

Off-Season
and
Pre-Season

Reps (10) or (5)

NAME:_____ DATE:_____ HGT:_____ WT:_____

POSITION:_____ VERTICAL JUMP: REACH | JUMP _____ CLASS:_____

INTERVAL 220 YARD SPRINTS:

WEEK #_____(1-8)

1._____   6._____   11._____

2._____   7._____   12._____

3._____   8._____   13._____

4._____   9._____   14._____

5._____   10._____   15._____

EXERCISES

PNF STRETCHING   WARM UP:

1. Bench Press: _____

2. Hip Sled/Squat: _____

3. Power Clean/High Pull: _____

4. Nautilus Leg Press: _____

5. Nautilus Leg Curl: _____

6. Flys:_____

7. Nautilus Pullover: _____

8. Nautilus Double Shoulder:_____

9. Concentration/Dumbell Row: _____

10. Seated Row/Shrugs:_____

11. Pulldowns-Neck-Chest _____

12. Cable Curls-Hammers:_____

13. Tricep Press/Pushdown: _____

14. Dips:_____ Chins: _____

15. PNF Stretching/Warm Down: _____

16. Ab Hangs:_____

REHABILITATION ROUTINE

INJURY: _____

EXERCISE: _____

WEIGHT/REPS:_____

FLEXIBILITIES: _____

COACHES COMMENTS: _____

Sheet #2
Cross Cty
&
Agilities

VIRGINIA
BASKETBALL

Off-Season
Pre-Season
Log

NAME:_____ DATE:_____ HGT:_____ WT:_____

| | R | J | |

POSITION:_____ VERTICAL JUMP_____ CLASS:_____

A. Cross Country Course: Time: _____

Distance: _____

B. Agilities: NAME/TIME   NAME/TIME

1._____   6. _____

2._____   7. _____

3._____   8. _____

4._____   9. _____

5._____   10. _____

PNF Stretching before and after workout.

Plus Abdominal Hangs.

C. **Quarterly Snapshot: DATE**

VIRGINIA BASKETBALL

**Sheet #3
In-Season
Heavy**

MAINTENANCE WORKOUT LOG

NAME:_____ DATE:_____ HGT:_____ WT:_____

POSITION:_____ CLASS:_____

EXERCISES

1. PNF Stretching/warm up with bar twists, jump rope (before & after).

2. Bench press, 3 X 3_____

3. Standing dumbell press, 2 X 3 _____

4. Incline flys (dumbells), 1 X 15 _____

5. AMF Hip Sled, 3 X 3 _____

6. Nautilus Leg curl & knee extension, 2 X 12 each_____

7. Thumbs up hammer curls, 3 X 10 _____

8. Cable Curls, 3 X 10 _____

9. Tricep Pushdowns 3 X 10_____ Cable kickback, 2 X 10 _____

10. Nautilus pullover, 1 X 10 _____

11. Seated Row, 1 X 10 _____

12. Pulldown to neck/chest, 1 X 10 _____

REHABILITATION ROUTINE

A. Injury: _____

B. Exercise(s): _____

C. Weight/Reps: _____

D. Flexibility (ies): _____

E. Coaches Comment: _____

3. Standing dumbell press, 2 X 3 _____

VIRGINIA BASKETBALL

**Sheet #4
In-Season
Light
(circuit)**

NAME:_____ DATE:_____ HGT:_____ WT:_____

POSITION:_____ CLASS:_____

1. PNF Stretching—warm-up with bar twists (seated), jump rope, jog or practice

CIRCUIT

A. **BENCH PRESS**- 3x max or to failure in 30 seconds

   HIP SLED- 2x max or to failure in 30 seconds

	Bench Poundage	Sled Poundage
guards/frosh	115	240
forwards/centers	135	290

* This 1st set on the bench should be close grip (18″) and then two wide

A. wide (std) grip. Hip sled should end with calf raises each way x 20 reps,

B. **Dumbell Press** (standing) -2x10, slightly bent knees, explosive reps, heavy as possible. _____

C. **Flys**—on flat bench/feet up—1x15_____

D. **Nautilus knee extension/leg curl,** 1x10 on both _____

E. **High cable curls (both hands),** 2x max in 30 sec. _____

F. **Triceps**—(Pushdowns on lat machine)
   2x max in 30 seconds: 1._____ 2._____

G. **Abdominal Hangs:**—2 sets, one leg raise, one crunch-8 seconds each way— crunches to failure

H. **PNF stretch** /warm down

NO. ONE

Off-Season FOUNDATION PHASE (First 4-weeks)

	LIFT	B./P.	Inc. Dumbell Press	LIFT	P./C.	Full Squats	LIFT	B./P.	Inc. Dumbell Press	LIFT	P./C.	Full Squats
WEEK 1	MONDAY	1 2 3 4 5	1 2 3 4 5	TUESDAY	1 2 3 4 5	1 2 3 4 5	THURSDAY	1 2 3 4 5	1 2 3 4 5	FRIDAY	1 2 3 4 5	1 2 3 4 5
WEEK 2	MONDAY	1 2 3 4 5	1 2 3 4 5	TUESDAY	1 2 3 4 5	1 2 3 4 5	THURSDAY	1 2 3 4 5	1 2 3 4 5	FRIDAY	1 2 3 4 5	1 2 3 4 5
WEEK 3	MONDAY	1 2 3 4 5	1 2 3 4 5	TUESDAY	1 2 3 4 5	1 2 3 4 5	THURSDAY	1 2 3 4 5	1 2 3 4 5	FRIDAY	1 2 3 4 5	1 2 3 4 5
WEEK 4	MONDAY	1 2 3 4 5	1 2 3 4 5	TUESDAY	1 2 3 4 5	1 2 3 4 5	THURSDAY	1 2 3 4 5	1 2 3 4 5	FRIDAY	1 2 3 4 5	1 2 3 4 5

ALL SETS IN THIS PHASE ARE FOR 10 REPETITIONS

NAME:	DATE:	GOAL ACHIEVED:	YES NO

NO. TWO   Off-Season **PREPARATION PHASE**   (Second 4-weeks)

	LIFT	CHEST/LEGS B./P.	Inc. D/P	Full Squats	LIFT	BACK WORK POWER CLEANS	LIFT	CHEST/LEGS B./P.	Inc. D/P	Full Squats
WEEK 5	MONDAY	1 2 3 4 5			WEDNESDAY	1 2 3 4 5	FRIDAY	1 2 3 4 5		
WEEK 6	MONDAY	1 2 3 4 5			WEDNESDAY	1 2 3 4 5	FRIDAY	1 2 3 4 5		
WEEK 7	MONDAY	1 2 3 4 5			WEDNESDAY	1 2 3 4 5	FRIDAY	1 2 3 4 5		
WEEK 8	MONDAY	1 2 3 4 5			WEDNESDAY	1 2 3 4 5	FRIDAY	1 2 3 4 5		

ALL SETS IN THIS PHASE ARE FOR 5 REPETITIONS

NO. THREE Off-Season PRE-COMPETITION PHASE (Final 3-weeks)

	LIFT	CHEST/LEGS			LIFT	BACK WORK POWER CLEANS	LIFT	CHEST/LEGS		
		B./P.	Inc. D/P	Full Squats				B./P.	Inc. D/P	Full Squats
WEEK 9	MONDAY	1 2 3 4 5			WEDNESDAY	1 2 3 4 5	FRIDAY	1 2 3 4 5		
WEEK 10	MONDAY	1 2 3 4 5			WEDNESDAY	1 2 3 4 5	FRIDAY	1 2 3 4 5		
WEEK 11	MONDAY	1 2 3 4 5			WEDNESDAY	1 2 3 4 5	FRIDAY	1 2 3 4 5		

MAX- -OUT-	MONDAY	LIFTS 1 2 3	TUESDAY	LIFTS 1 2 3	THURSDAY	Conditioning Max Day	FRIDAY	Conditioning Max Day

ALL SETS IN THIS PHASE ARE FOR 3 REPETITIONS
(EXCEPT MAX-OUT, WHICH IS FOR ONE REP)

NO. ONE Off-Season **FOUNDATION PHASE** (First 4-weeks)

	LIFT	B./P.	Inc. Dumbell Press	LIFT	P./C.	Full Squats	LIFT	B./P.	Inc. Dumbell Press	LIFT	P./C.	Full Squats
WEEK 1	MONDAY	1 135 x 10	1 40 x 10	TUESDAY	1 135 x 10	1 135 x 10	THURSDAY	1 135 x 10	1 40 x 10	FRIDAY	1 135 x 10	1 135 x 10
		2 145 x 10	2 40 x 10		2 135 x 10	2 165 x 10		2 145 x 10	2 40 x 10		2 135 x 10	2 165 x 10
		3 155 x 10	3 40 x 10		3 145 x 10	3 185 x 10		3 155 x 10	3 40 x 10		3 145 x 10	3 185 x 10
		4 160 x 10	4 40 x 10		4 155 x 10	4 215 x 10		4 160 x 10	4 40 x 10		4 155 x 10	4 215 x 10
		5 165 x 10	5 40 x 10		5 165 x 10	5 225 x 10		5 165 x 10	5 40 x 10		5 165 x 10	5 225 x 10
WEEK 2	MONDAY	1 135 x 10	1 40 x 10	TUESDAY	1 135 x 10	1 135 x 10	THURSDAY	1 135 x 10	1 40 x 10	FRIDAY	1 135 x 10	1 135 x 10
		2 155 x 10	2 40 x 10		2 135 x 10	2 165 x 10		2 155 x 10	2 40 x 10		2 135 x 10	2 165 x 10
		3 165 x 10	3 40 x 10		3 150 x 10	3 195 x 10		3 165 x 10	3 40 x 10		3 150 x 10	3 195 x 10
		4 170 x 10	4 40 x 10		4 160 x 10	4 220 x 10		4 170 x 10	4 40 x 10		4 160 x 10	4 220 x 10
		5 175 x 10	5 40 x 10		5 170 x 10	5 230 x 10		5 175 x 10	5 50 x 10		5 170 x 10	5 230 x 10
WEEK 3	MONDAY	1 135 x 10	1 40 x 10	TUESDAY	1 135 x 10	1 135 x 10	THURSDAY	1 135 x 10	1 40 x 10	FRIDAY	1 135 x 10	1 135 x 10
		2 160 x 10	2 40 x 10		2 135 x 10	2 180 x 10		2 160 x 10	2 40 x 10		2 135 x 10	2 180 x 10
		3 165 x 10	3 50 x 10		3 155 x 10	3 205 x 10		3 165 x 10	3 50 x 10		3 155 x 10	3 205 x 10
		4 170 x 10	4 50 x 10		4 165 x 10	4 230 x 10		4 170 x 10	4 50 x 10		4 165 x 10	4 230 x 10
		5 180 x 10	5 50 x 10		5 175 x 10	5 240 x 10		5 180 x 10	5 50 x 10		5 175 x 10	5 240 x 10
WEEK 4	MONDAY	1 135 x 10	1 40 x 10	TUESDAY	1 135 x 10	1 135 x 10	THURSDAY	1 135 x 10	1 40 x 10	FRIDAY	1 135 x 10	1 135 x 10
		2 165 x 10	2 50 x 10		2 135 x 10	2 185 x 10		2 165 x 10	2 50 x 10		2 135 x 10	2 185 x 10
		3 170 x 10	3 50 x 10		3 165 x 10	3 215 x 10		3 170 x 10	3 50 x 10		3 165 x 10	3 215 x 10
		4 175 x 10	4 50 x 10		4 175 x 10	4 240 x 10		4 175 x 10	4 50 x 10		4 175 x 10	4 240 x 10
		5 185 x 10	5 50 x 10		5 185 x 10	5 250 x 10		5 185 x 10	5 50 x 10		5 185 x 10	5 250 x 10

ALL SETS IN THIS PHASE ARE FOR 10 REPETITIONS

NAME: SAMPSON, R.   DATE: Summer Cycle-82   GOAL ACHIEVED: YES

NO. TWO   Off-Season   PREPARATION PHASE   (Second 4-weeks)

	LIFT	CHEST/LEGS B./P.	Inc. D/P	Full Squats	LIFT	BACK WORK POWER CLEANS	LIFT	CHEST/LEGS B./P.	Inc. D/P	Full Squats
WEEK 5	MONDAY	1 135 x 10	40 x 10	135 x 10	WEDNESDAY	1 135 x 5	FRIDAY	1 135 x 10	40 x 10	135 x 10
		2 200 x 5	50 x 5	205 x 5		2 140 x 5		2 200 x 5	50 x 5	205 x 5
		3 205 x 5	50 x 5	240 x 5		3 170 x 5		3 205 x 5	50 x 5	240 x 5
		4 210 x 5	60 x 5	260 x 5		4 205 x 5		4 210 x 5	60 x 5.	260 x 5
		5 215 x 5	60 x 5	275 x 5		5 220 x 5		5 215 x 5	60 x 5	275 x 5
WEEK 6	MONDAY	1 135 x 10	50 x 10	135 x 10	WEDNESDAY	1 135 x 5	FRIDAY	1 135 x 10	50 x 10	135 x 10
		2 205 x 5	60 x 5	225 x 5		2 140 x 5		2 205 x 5	60 x 5	225 x 5
		3 210 x 5	60 x 5	250 x 5		3 175 x 5		3 210 x 5	60 x 5	250 x 5
		4 215 x 5	60 x 5	270 x 5		4 210 x 5		4 215 x 5	60 x 5	270 x 5
		5 220 x 5	60 x 5	285 x 5		5 225 x 5		5 220 x 5	60 x 5	285 x 5
WEEK 7	MONDAY	1 135 x 10	60 x 10	135 x 10	WEDNESDAY	1 135 x 5	FRIDAY	1 135 x 10	60 x 10	135 x 10
		2 210 x 5	70 x 5	225 x 5		2 140 x 5		2 210 x 5	70 x 5	225 x 5
		3 215 x 5	70 x 5	255 x 5		3 185 x 5		3 215 x 5	70 x 5	255 x 5
		4 220 x 5	70 x 5	275 x 5		4 215 x 5		4 220 x 5	70 x 5	275 x 5
		5 225 x 5	70 x 5	290 x 5		5 230 x 5		5 225 x 5	70 x 5	290 x 5
WEEK 8	MONDAY	1 135 x 10	60 x 5	135 x 10	WEDNESDAY	1 135 x 5	FRIDAY	1 135 x 10	60 x 5	135 x 10
		2 190 x 5	70 x 5	225 x 5		2 145 x 5		2 190 x 5	70 x 5	225 x 5
		3 205 x 5	70 x 5	260 x 5		3 190 x 5		3 205 x 5	70 x 5	260 x 5
		4 220 x 5	70 x 5	280 x 5		4 220 x 5		4 220 x 5	70 x 5	280 x 5
		5 230 x 5	80 x 5	295 x 5		5 235 x 5		5 230 x 5	80 x 5	295 x 5

ALL SETS IN THIS PHASE ARE FOR 5 REPETITIONS

NAME: SAMPSON, R.   **DATE:** Summer Cycle-82   **GOAL ACHIEVED:** **YES**

NO. THREE   Off-Season   PRE-COMPETITION PHASE (Final 3-weeks)

	LIFT	CHEST/LEGS B./P.	Inc. D/P	Full Squats	LIFT	BACK WORK POWER CLEANS	LIFT	CHEST/LEGS B./P.	Inc. D/P	Full Squats
WEEK 9	MONDAY	1 135 x 10	60 x 3	135 x 10	WEDNESDAY	Warm-Up 135 x 5 1 155 x 3	FRIDAY	1 135 x10	60 x 3	135 x 10
		2 210 x 3	70 x 3	225 x 3		2 175 x 3		2 210 x 3	70 x 3	225 x 3
		3 225 x 3	70 x 3	265 x 3		3 195 x 3		3 225 x 3	70 x 3	265 x 3
		4 235 x 3	80 x 3	285 x 3		4 225 x 3		4 235 x 3	80 x 3	285 x 3
		5 240 x 3	80 x 3	305 x 3		5 245 x 3		5 240 x 3	80 x 3	305 x 3
WEEK 10	MONDAY	1 135 x 10	70 x 3	135 x 10	WEDNESDAY	Warm-up 135 x 5 1 160 x 3	FRIDAY	1 135 x 10	70 x 3	135 x 10
		2 225 x 3	70 x 3	230 x 3		2 180 x 3		2 225 x 3	70 x 3	230 x 3
		3 235 x 3	80 x 3	270 x 3		3 200 x 3		3 235 x 3	80 x 3	270 x 3
		4 240 x 3	80 x 3	290 x 3		4 230 x 3		4 240 x 3	80 x 3	290 x 3
		5 245 x 3	90 x 3	310 x 3		5 250 x 3		5 245 x 3	90 x 3	310 x 3
WEEK 11	MONDAY	1 135 x 10	70 x 3	135 x 10	WEDNESDAY	Warm-up 135 x 5 1 165 x 3	FRIDAY	1 135 x 10	70 x 3	135 x 10
		2 230 x 3	80 x 3	235 x 3		2 185 x 3		2 230 x 3	80 x 3	235 x 3
		3 240 x 3	80 x 3	275 x 3		3 205 x 3		3 240 x 3	80 x 3	275 x 3
		4 245 x 3	90 x 3	295 x 3		4 235 x 3		4 245 x 3	90 x 3	295 x 3
		5 250 x 3	90 x 3	315 x 3		5 255 x 3		5 250 x 3	90 x 3	315 x 3

| **MAX- -OUT-** | MONDAY | **LIFTS**
1 Bench Press
265 x 1
2 Inc. D/P
100 x 1
3 Hammer Curls
90 x 10 (each) | TUESDAY | **LIFTS**
1 Power Clean
265 x 1
2 Squat
325 x 1
3 Hip Sled
690 x 3 | THURSDAY | Conditioning Max Day | FRIDAY | Conditioning Max Day |

ALL SETS IN THIS PHASE ARE FOR 3 REPETITIONS
(EXCEPT MAX-OUT, WHICH IS FOR ONE REP)

GLOSSARY OF STRENGTH TRAINING TERMS

Abs—Abreviation for the abdominal muscle group.

Adipose tissue—fat tissue.

Aerobic—Adjective meaning "in the presence of oxygen."

Amino acids—nitrogen-containing compounds that form the building blocks of proteins.

Anabolic—"Tissue-building"—i.e., conducive to the constructive process of metabolism, as opposed to "catabolic," which means "breaking down."

Anaerobic—Adjective meaning "in the absence of oxygen."

Androgenic—characterized by the development of secondary sex characteristics in the male.

Barbell—a weight used for strength training, composed of two discs connected by a steel bar, usually 5'–7' long.

Bench press—one of the major powerlifts.

Biopsy—removal and examination of human tissue.

Body composition—various components making up the human body—mainly fat and tissue that is fat-free.

Bulking up—the act of increasing bodyweight by adding both fat and muscle density.

Burning—working (exercising) a muscle to the point where lactic acid buildup causes a "burning" sensation.

Calorie—unit of work (or energy) which equals the heat necessary to raise the temperature of one gram of water by 1°C.

Carbohydrate—chemical compound containing carbon, hydrogen, and oxygen; one of the basic foodstuffs, usually referred to as sugars, starches, and celluloses.

Cardiorespiratory—form of physical conditioning to strengthen the heart and blood vessels.

Central nervous system—the portion of the nervous system consisting of the brain and spinal cord.

Cheating—handling too much weight (or using improper form) in an exercise, thereby relying on surrounding muscle groups to assist in the movement.

Circuit training—a form of conditioning that involves moving from one "station" to another for a prescribed number of sets and reps, usually for a prescribed "time" as well, then moving on to another.

Clean & jerk—one of the "Olympic" lifts.

Connective tissue—the support tissues that bind the various body parts together.

Cool-down—any exercise procedure, usually stretching, performed after strenuous exercise and designed to lower (or remove) lactic acid build-up from the muscles and blood.

Cutting up—the act of developing more muscularity, achieved by a combination of extreme diet and exercise.

Cycle training—also known as "Periodization," referring to year-round training and long-range planning.

Dead lift—one of three power lifts.

Delts—an abbreviation for the deltoids: denoting the large triangular muscle of the shoulder which raises the arm away from the side.

Dumbbell—two plates (or metal balls) joined by a short bar, about eight to ten inches long; usually held in one hand.

Eccentric contraction—muscular contraction in which the muscle lengthens under stress.

Endurance (aerobic) training—a form of conditioning designed to increase aerobic capacity and the endurance base.

Energy—the capacity or ability to perform work.

Energy balance—a state of equilibrium between caloric expenditure and calorie intake.

Ergogenic—the act of improving work or energy performance.

Failure—(a) to miss a lift. (b) "To go beyond failure" means to force out one or more repetitions after the last successful rep, usually with the help of a training partner (see "forced repetitions" below).

Fast-twitch fiber—muscle fiber characterized by fast contraction time, high anaerobic capacity, and low aerobic capacity; the type of muscle fiber most suitable for high-power output activities.

Fat—(a) a foodstuff that contains fatty acids and glycerol. (b) The soft tissue in the body other than that making up the skeletal muscle mass and the viscera.

Fatigue—a state of discomfort, weariness, and decreased efficiency resulting from prolonged or excessive effort and exertion.

Flex—to bend or curve the arm to contract or extend (and tighten) a muscle.

Flexibility—the range of motion about a joint (static flexibility); opposition or resistance of a joint to motion (dynamic flexibility).

Flush—to cleanse a muscle by increasing the blood supply to the muscle; removing various poisons left in the muscle by exertion.

Forced breathing—taking very large breaths of air that force the rib cage to expand.

Forced repetitions—performing additional work (repetitions) once the muscle or muscle group cannot complete the movement on its own.

Free fall—letting a weight drop without resisting its movement.

Glucose—sugar.

Go-for-max—referring to the desire to attempt a maximum lift for any number of repetitions.

Golgi tendon organ—a proproreceptor located within the muscle tendon.

Hamstring—any of the tendons of the thigh muscle at the back of the knee.

Hand-off—the act of assisting someone in getting a poundage in the proper lifting position before beginning the exercise.

Heart rate—the number of times the heart beats per minute.

Hypertrophy—excessive growth of a muscle.

Interval training—exercise program whereby the body is subjected to short but repeated periods of stress interspersed with rest periods.

Isokinetic contraction—contraction of muscles performed at a constant speed and in such a fashion that the tension developed by the muscle while shortening is maximal over the entire range of motion.

Isometric contraction—muscle contraction in which tension is developed but with no change in muscle length. Usually pushing and pulling against an immovable object. Also referred to as "static contraction."

Kilocalorie—unit of energy or of work equal to the amount of heat necessary to raise the temperature of one kilogram of water 1°C.

Kilogram—metric unit of weight equalling 2.2 pounds.

Lactic acid—a fatiguing metabolite of the "lactic acid system" resulting from an incomplete carbohydrate breakdown.

Lats—an abbreviation for latissimus dorsi, a large muscle of the back that draws the arm downward, backward, and rotates it.

Lay-off—taking a break from training.

Lean body weight—that portion of the body weight remaining when the weight of body fat is subtracted from the total body weight.

Lifting belt—thick leather belt specifically designed for support of the lower back.

Lock-out—the last portion of any exercise movement resulting in straightened arms or legs or torso, completing the exercise.

Loose weights—also known as "free weights," referring

either to barbells as opposed to machines, or to extra plates that are available for increasing the poundage.

Max-out—going for maximum poundage in a certain lift (same as "go-for-max").

Maximal oxygen consumption (VO₂ max)—the maximal rate at which oxygen can be consumed per minute; the power or capacity of the aerobic (oxygen) system.

Metabolism—the sum total of the chemical changes or reactions that occur in the body.

Muscle-bound—a colloquial term meaning "lacking in flexibility." The term is a misnomer when applied to persons adhering to the Virginia System of Strength Training and Conditioning because such persons are definitely not lacking in flexibility.

Muscle endurance—ability of a muscle or group of muscles to perform repeated contractions against any given load for an extended period of time.

Nerve—a cord-like structure that conveys impulses from one part of the body to another.

Nutrition—the process of assimilating food.

Olympic lifts—two highly technical lifts performed by specialists in Olympic weightlifting, consisting of the clean & jerk and the snatch.

Overload—the act of exercising a muscle or muscle group against resistance greater than that which is normally encountered.

Overtrain—when the exercise program has become too strenuous or monotonous, causing a loss of muscle size, strength, and/or mental drive (intensity).

Partial repetitions—exercising without moving the resistance through a full range of motion, not making a complete contraction or extension of the muscle being exercised.

Pecs—abbreviation for "pectoralis," the major muscle of the chest.

Power lifts—three lifting movements consisting of the squat, bench press, and dead lift, all performed competitively.

Progressive resistance—overloading a muscle or muscle group on a consistent basis throughout the duration of the training program.

Quadriceps, or quads—largest thigh muscle.

Repetitions—the act of performing an exercise repeatedly.

Receptor—a sense organ that receives stimuli.

Reflex—an automatic response induced by stimulation of a receptor.

Repetition maximum (RM)—the maximum load that a muscle can lift in a given set before fatigue (failure) sets in.

Set—a fixed number of repetitions, making up one "set."

Second wind—a sensation characterized by a transition from fatigue during exercise to a more comfortable and energetic feeling.

Skinfold—a pinch of skin and subcutaneous fat from which total body fat may be estimated accurately. A caliper is the device usually used to measure this body fat content.

Snatch—highly technical Olympic lift in which the weight bar is raised from the floor above the head in one continuous movement.

Specificity—in terms of conditioning, the act of exercising in such a way as to closely duplicate the movements of a particular sport skill movement.

Spinera erector—important muscle in the lower back.

Squat—one of the "power lifts."

Sticking point—(a) the point beyond which a weight cannot be moved in a certain exercise. (b) The halting of progress in adding weight regularly on any given exercise.

Steroid—generally, any of a large group of fat-soluble compounds, usually with anabolic characteristics (building up tissue); more specifically, derivative of the male sex hormone testosterone, which has masculinizing properties.

Strength—the maximum pulling or pushing force of a muscle or muscle group.

Super set—alternating back and forth between two or more exercises with little or no rest in between, until the prescribed number of sets are completed.

Training—any program of conditioning designed to improve the skills and increase the energy capacity of an athlete engaged in a particular sport.

Training partner—one who exercises along with another on a conditioning program.

Wraps—materials used to give support to joints. Examples are knee wraps, wrist wraps, and lifting belts.

INDEX